Brody's Regent Review:
American History 2018

Regent Review in less than 100 pages

M. Brody M.A. ED

© 2018 Moshe Brody

It is forbidden by federal and local law to copy in any format any page from this book without the express permission of the author.

For all comments and questions please email:

brodysregentreview@gmail.com

To purchase your copy-please go to Amazon.com and search for Brody's Regent Review Table of Contents

Table of Contents

Chapter 1	Pre-US Life	6
Chapter 2	Slavery Issues	8
Chapter 3	Democratic foundations	9
Chapter 4	Revolutionary Rumblings	12
Chapter 5	Revolution!	15
Chapter 6	From Revolution to Statehood	18
Chapter 7	The Constitution: the legislative branch	21
Chapter 8	The Constitution: the executive branch	24
Chapter 9	The Constitution: the judicial branch	27
Chapter 10	Post Constitutional America-1791-1820's	32
Chapter 11	America 1810-1830	37
Chapter 12	Reform, Growth and Civil War: America 1830's-1860's	40
Chapter 13	Reconstruction (1865-1877)	45
Chapter 14	The growth of American business 1880-1920	50
Chapter 15	Urbanization and immigration: 1880's-1920's	53
Chapter 16	The Progressive movement: 1880's-1920's	57
Chapter 17	The imperialistic age: 1880's-1920's	62
Chapter 18	WWI and the interwar years 1917-1941	67
Chapter 19	The New Deal and WWII: 1930's-1945	71
Chapter 20	The Cold war: 1947-1991	77
Chapter 21	1945-1975: economic, social and cultural change	82
Chapter 22	The last forty years: 1975-2005	89
Fifteen Supreme Court decisions		90
Answer Key for Regent's questions		95

CHAPTER 1
Pre-US Life

Pre-US Life

1) America was originally settled by Native Americans who preceded the colonists by thousands of years. (Some theorize that they came here from Asia during the last Ice age). By the time colonists came in the 1500's, Native Americans had spread across the breadth of the country and lived largely as hunter-gatherer societies hunting big game especially Bison in the Great Plains. However when white settlers came, conflict became inevitable as the Europeans brought over their agricultural lifestyle to America and began to fence off large tracts of land for their farms. These lands had previously been open and free areas shared by beast and man and now became settled areas with large fields made ready for planting. Another way that colonists impacted Native American life was that they unintentionally killed out large amounts of the native population through epidemics they brought with them such as smallpox and other diseases. While the Europeans had immunity from Europe, these native tribes had never experienced these diseases. Therefore they suffered great declines in population when they came in contact with white settlers.

2) Colonialism: As time moved on, émigrés from Holland, England, France and Spain settled different parts of the US. The Dutch abandoned their colonial efforts in the US in the 1600's while the French settled down in small settlements trapping fur in the large Midwest, Northeast and parts of Canada. The Spanish settled parts of the South and southwest stretching from Mexico to California. The English settled on the eastern seaboard, east of the Appalachian Mountains. The English colonies could be divided geographically and economically.

3) The Colonies: The Colonies had three regions: the Northern Colonies, the Middle Colonies and the Southern Colonies. The Northern Colonies, such as New England and Rohde Island, had poor soil and served as the port for incoming and outgoing goods (mainly to England where the colonies served as a mercantile colony meant to enrich the mother country). The Middle Colonies such as New York and New Jersey served as ports but also had some agriculture too. The Southern Colonies had fertile land and was mainly used for agriculture (farming).

4) Reasons for early immigration: Immigrants came here from England for 3 reasons:

a. **Economic:** people saw economic benefits in settling in a new land in which they could grow and prosper.

b. **Religious:** people such as the Puritans, Quakers, and Pilgrims all felt at odds with the religious establishment in England and wished to escape the tyranny of the majority.

c. **Political:** people whose views were oppressed in England saw an opportunity in America to live by their ideals that they believed in, away from the oppressive atmosphere in Europe.

REGENTS REVIEW

1. The original settlements in the thirteen British colonies were all located
    (1) east of the Appalachian Mountains
    (2) along the Gulf Coast
    (3) on the Great Plains
    (4) west of the Mississippi River

2. What was a main reason large plantations developed in the South during the colonial period?
    (1) British laws discouraged tenant farming.
    (2) Cotton could only be grown in wetlands.
    (3) Southern mountains led to the development of isolated, self-sufficient farms.
    (4) The coastal plain in the South contained large areas of fertile soil.

3. During the colonial period, goods were most commonly transported on
    (1) rivers   (3) railroads
    (2) canals   (4) turnpikes

CHAPTER 2
Slavery Issues

Reasons for slavery in America

5) The decimation of the Native American population through the spread of diseases left large plantation owners with few laborers. The Northern Colonies which relied on shipping and trade for their livelihoods had little need for labor. However, the South and to a lesser extent the Middle Colonies were heavily dependent on labor, and so they sought out another source of cheap labor.

The Slave Trade

6) American farmers looked to African slaves for cheap labor. Colonists went to Africa and captured slaves and brought them back to the Colonies. On the way to the Americas, slaves were packed into boats with inadequate food, water, or shelter. Overcrowding and unsanitary living led to the spread of disease which caused many African American slaves to die on the way. This transfer across the sea is known as the middle passage. The slave trade was also part of the larger Columbian exchange (also called triangular trade since three continents were involved in the trade-Africa, Europe, and the Americas) in which large amounts goods were shipped in many directions.

REGENTS REVIEW

1. **In the 1700s, the triangular trade led directly to the**
    (1) middle colonies' role as the chief importers of agricultural products
    (2) rapid industrialization of the southern colonies
    (3) decline of the New England economy
    (4) increased importation of enslaved Africans to the Western Hemisphere

CHAPTER 3
Democratic Foundations

7) At the time that America was founded, there were already five historical precedents that the founding fathers could look to for guidance in creating their own form of democratic government.

a. **Greek democracy:** the Greeks had created their own direct democracy where citizens of Athens voted on all public issues.

b. **Roman Republic:** the Romans overthrew their Etruscan overlords in the 500 BCE and promised they would never again be ruled by a king. Instead they established a Republic in which citizens would elect Senators which would vote on all issues. In addition they had two Consuls which would run the state for them and a Dictator during the times of war.

c. **Magna Carta:** during the 1200's, the King of England made a big mistake by going to war without his Nobles' permission. When the Nobles revolted, the King went to war with them and lost, resulting in his forced writing of a document called the Magna Carta. This document stated that going forward, in addition to the guaranteeing of some basic civil rights, the King would have to consult with the Lords before he could go to war and embark on other national projects which required money.

d. **Petition of right:** In 1625 King James of England's son, Charles I, took over. He inherited his father's absolutist ways and ignored the parliament. When he wanted money and went to the Parliament to get it, they agreed to provide the money as long as he would sign the Petition of right. The petition said that the king can't imprison anyone for no reason or collect taxes without asking parliament first. He signed it and then closed Parliament for 11 years. This would eventually lead to the English Civil War.

e. **English Bill of Rights:** When William and Mary were invited to become King and Queen, the country made them accept the English Bill of Rights. This bill promised the following points:

- The Monarch has to summon parliament regularly – Limited Monarchy
- Give parliament power of the purse-the power to decide which projects would be funded
- The King or Queen cannot interfere or suspend laws made by the parliament
- Citizens cannot be excessively fined, no cruel and unusual punishment, a trial by a jury, the right of Habeas Corpus - people have to charged with a crime to be held in prison.

Enlightenment influences

8) Besides these historical precedents, the spirit of Enlightenment had swept through America as well. The American people were captivated by four thinkers in particular. They were: Locke, Rousseau, Voltaire, and Montesquieu. Let us examine the theories of each thinker:

a. **John Locke:** John Locke argued that people are afraid of other people who will come and grab away their life or liberty or/and property. (This is despite the fact that Locke held a positive view of humankind). Because of this fear, people gathered together to protect themselves and their property, and this is the reason why people formed governments. Hence the best gov't is the weakest, but one that protects an individual's, life, liberty and property. If the government was to become too powerful and not protect these three rights, then it is the right of the people to overthrow the government and start anew. This concept is called the Social Contract and is the foundation of Declaration of Independence.

b. **Rousseau:** said that people are inherently good but society makes them bad because it corrupts their natural self which is good. Hence no government is good, but if one is needed, it can be tolerated if the basis of the government is the people and it is for the people. This then is the cornerstone of Popular Sovereignty - the control of the government by the people.

c. **Voltaire** wrote many critical and objectionable things but said that despite the possible objectionable content, every person's views ought to be allowed to be heard and allowed to be expressed. This formed the basis of freedom of speech and press.

d. **Baron de Montesquieu** wrote that the success of the British government was its separation of powers between legislative, judicial, and executive branches. He said the resulting balance of power is the best way to protect against tyranny.

9) Finally in America there were already nascent beginnings of democracy starting to sprout in the Colonies. They were the Mayflower Compact and the Virginia House of Burgesses.

a. **Mayflower compact:** was a document signed by the Pilgrims on the Mayflower. It contains an oath amongst themselves stating that when they landed in America, they would ensure that all decisions would be handled using democratic means. Thus the Plymouth Colony was founded on democratic concepts.

b. **The Virginia House of Burgesses:** was the parliament of the state of Virginia and conducted itself in a democratic manner. Thus one of the main states before the revolution was already a practicing democracy before we functioned as a democracy.

REGENTS REVIEW

1. In colonial America, the House of Burgesses, the Mayflower Compact, and town hall meetings were all developments that led to the
   (1) regulation of trade with Native American Indians
   (2) protection of the rights of women
   (3) elimination of the power of the upper classes
   (4) creation of representative government (aug. `12, 5)

2. Which document is most closely associated with John Locke's social contract theory of government?
   (1) Albany Plan of Union
   (2) Declaration of Independence
   (3) Treaty of Paris (1783)
   (4) Sedition Act of 1798 (June, `12, 3

3. The writings of John Locke, Jean-Jacques Rousseau, and Baron de Montesquieu are significant in United States history because they (Jan `12, 5)
   (1) opposed the use of slave labor in the Americas
   (2) supported the absolute right of the king to impose taxes
   (3) encouraged the formation of political parties and political machines
   (4) influenced the authors of the Declaration of Independence and the Constitution

4. The right of habeas corpus establishes the principle that
   (1) people accused of a crime have a right to a lawyer
   (2) all punishments for crimes should be reasonable
   (3) a person should not be forced to be a witness against himself
   (4) no person should be held in custody unless charged with a crime

5. Which heading best completes the partial outline below?
   I. _____
     A. Mayflower Compact
     B. House of Burgesses
     C. New England town meetings
   (1) Attempts to Overthrow British Rule
   (2) Development of Self-Government in the American Colonies
   (3) Establishment of British Parliamentary Control Over the Colonies
   (4) Social Reform Movements in the American Colonies

CHAPTER 4
Revolutionary Rumblings

10) At first, colonies were allowed to trade unregulated by the English government. The British had a mercantilist policy (a colonial economic policy in which the mother country would acquire raw materials from the colony and ship back to the colonies manufactured goods) towards their colonies and wished for stability. To achieve that goal, the British government generally let the colonists run their own affairs under a policy called Salutary Neglect (a healthy ignoring of the colonies). This was good for both sides since it kept the colonists happy by giving them a sense that they were in charge, and the English happy who benefitted from stable colonies. Despite this arrangement, colonists felt a sense of inferiority in relation to their British overlords, and lacked a sense of equality with their British peers. This sense of inferiority may have contributed feelings of resentment long before the conflict with Britain began.

11) This period of peace began to crumble in the aftermath of the French-Indian War (1754-1763). The war, which was waged against the French in Europe and America, ended with a victory for the British. Although the colonists took part in the fighting, they were prohibited by the British government from settling in conquered territory west of the Appalachian Mountains under the proclamation of 1763. The goal of the proclamation was to keep the peace with the Indian tribes in that area and thereby lower the defense costs of the British government.

12) This policy created some tension between the colonists and their government by placing what they perceived as unnecessary restrictions on their settlement activities. This resentment though was minimal compared to the anger directed at the British government after the King placed taxes on them in order to refill the coffers of the treasury following the war. Even more disturbing to the colonists was the stationing of the British troops in the colonies after the war in order to maintain the peace with French. Despite being a small amount of money, the colonists felt that it was unfair to be taxed without being asked beforehand (thus the catchphrase of the time "no taxation without representation"). An example of such a tax was the stamp tax which demanded that all printed materials produced in the colonies be printed upon special paper stamped with a tax seal (which they had to pay for). Another was the sugar tax and the currency tax which regulated the paper money of the colonies. These acts all served to increase the fury

of the colonists at the royal government. Many boycotted royal goods and in some instances even incited violence directed at the offices of the government in the colonies.

13) As time moved on, the situation worsened. The British government issued new decrees such as the Townshend acts, which placed a tax on many basic staples of life, and people began a protest against the British government. The protesters surrounded a group of English soldiers in Boston and began throwing rocks and snowballs at them. The soldiers responded by firing at the crowd, killing 11 and leading to even more anger at the government. This was later termed the Boston Massacre. News about the massacre was spread through an inaccurate depiction by artist Paul Revere, who used the incident to fan the flames against the British. Later on, colonists dressed as Native Americans boarded English ships laden with tea and threw the tea into the harbor and which eventually became known as the Boston tea party.

14) This incident led the British government to pass a series of restrictions and punishments on the colonists called the coercive acts, (or the intolerable acts by the colonists). Among the punishments was that the Boston Harbor was to be closed until the colonists repaid them for the tea they lost in the Boston tea party, and the quartering acts which demanded that the colonists quarter, or house, British soldiers in their homes.

15) At this point the colonists began to mobilize against the government. Inflammatory papers were written and distributed advocating rebellion against the royal government. However, not everyone was for the rebellion. Many people, called loyalists, were on the side of the British and wanted to see a resolution hammered out by the parties. They were opposed to the acts of violence such as Tarring and Feathering which were carried out by Patriots (people who opposed the British crown). Over time, public opinion turned against the loyalists. Fiery pamphlets such as Thomas Paine's Common Sense, and others swayed the public into taking sides and action (although Pains' book only came out after the war had broken out). Colonists assembled to discuss their next moves and to respond to the intolerable acts in what became known as the first continental Congress.

16) At the Congress, a whole host of opinions were expressed on the next course of action. Some suggested a total boycott of British goods, while others suggested that they train their own militias. They also expressed their rights and grievances and petitioned the King to address their complaints.

17) When King George heard about the desire to train the militia, he sensed a rebellion and ordered more military to the US. When the troops arrived in America, a garrison of troops left for Concord New England to arrest militia members and their weapons. Paul Revere got wind of it and spread the news around that the British were coming. Members of the Massachusetts militia met them and were ordered by the British troops to back off. While they walked back a shot rang out from among the militia members and thus the American Revolution began.

REGENTS REVIEW

1. **Which statement about the British colonial policy of mercantilism is most accurate?**

    (1) Raw materials from the colonies were shipped to England.
    (2) England encouraged the colonies to seek independence.
    (3) The colonies were required to send manufactured goods to Europe.
    (4) The British opposed the use of slave labor in the colonies. (Aug. `12, 4, 6)

2. **During the early 1770s, how did the British government respond to increasing American protests of British colonial policy?**

    (1) It offered self-government to the colonists.
    (2) It increased efforts to maintain order and enforce laws.
    (3) It agreed to grant the colonies representation in Parliament.
    (4) It asked France for help in controlling the Colonists

3. **In the publication Common Sense, Thomas Paine argued that**

    (1) foreign nations would reject an independent American government
    (2) the British government would be impossible to overthrow
    (3) America was dependent on British trade and protection
    (4) the American colonies should break away from England

4. **American colonists showed their opposition to the British taxation and trade restrictions of the 1760s primarily by**

    (1) supporting the French against the British
    (2) boycotting products from Great Britain
    (3) overthrowing the royal governors in most of the colonies
    (4) purchasing additional products from Native American Indian tribes

CHAPTER 5
Revolution!

18) With the potential of a major conflict on the horizon, Congress met again in Philadelphia to discuss what should be done next. They appointed George Washington as the commander in chief of the new war effort and then proceeded to write a letter of reconciliation to the King as a last ditch effort at saving the colonies from going to war with its mother country. This became known as the Olive branch Petition. The effort was too little and too late, and by the time it was received in England, the King refused to accept it. Instead, he signed a Declaration of Rebellion and ordered his troops to suppress it. The assembled congress met to lead the war effort. This Congress was called the Second Continental Congress.

War!

19) After the clash in Concord, called the Battle of Lexington and Concord, a call went out to all the colonies to send their militias to fight the British in and around Boston. They responded and the second major battle began with Battle of Bunker Hill. This was a hill surrounding Boston which the British tried to capture from the colonial forces. Being that the colonial forces had the advantage of being on the top of the hill, they succeeded at inflicting great losses upon the British. While the victory was short lived, since the British were able to take back the hill after the patriots ran out of ammunition, the small victory of the colonists shocked the British establishment back home as they came to terms with the surprising strength of colonists. It was at this time that Thomas Paine's Common Sense appeared and helped swing the colonists into joining the revolution.

Declaration of Independence

20) Declaration of Independence: In July 1776, while the hostilities were just beginning, the Second Continental Congress met and drafted a Declaration of Independence from England. The document is more than just a formal declaration of independence for it includes

1) a theory of government,

2) a list of grievances (complaints) against King George (i.e. the reasons why they feel correct for breaking away) and

3) finally a declaration of independence.

Articles of Confederation

21) Articles of Confederation: The war raged on for 6 years until in 1781 the British finally surrendered at Yorktown. In 1783, a formal peace treaty was signed by the British called the Treaty of Paris. During the war, the colonies signed a paper called the Articles of Confederation in which they formally joined together in a loose union. The Confederation was not ratified until 1781 although it was originally drafted in 1776-7. The main goal of the articles was to create a weak central government. This was so due to the fact that the colonists feared creating a strong central government that would strip its rights just as the government in England tried to do. Thus despite its drawbacks and limitations, it was the set of principles that were agreed upon by the colonists at the time.

22) Successes of the Articles of confederation:

a. ended the American Revolution with the successful negotiation of the Treaty of Paris that set the borders of the US at the Mississippi river.

b. Passed the Northwest Ordinance act in 1787 which gave the necessary conditions for new states to enter the Union and prohibited slavery in the Northwest Territory.

23) Weaknesses of the A of C:

a. no single currency was established so business was hampered

b. Congress was weak because they could not directly tax the individual and had to be at the mercy of the state to tax

c. No President

d. Government could not raise money to pay for an army so it was a vulnerable to attack both internally and externally.

REGENTS REVIEW

1. The writers of the Constitution corrected an economic weakness under the Articles of Confederation when they

    (1) granted Congress the power to levy and collect taxes
    (2) created an executive branch headed by the President
    (3) granted the President the authority to negotiate treaties
    (4) created a two-house legislature (June `12,

2. The primary purpose of the Articles of Confederation was to (Jan `12, 3,4)

    (1) provide revenues for the national government
    (2) establish the basic framework of the national government
    (3) give the national government the power to regulate interstate commerce
    (4) guarantee a bill of rights to protect citizens from the national government

3. The Northwest Ordinance of 1787 established a model for later settlement by providing for the

    (1) legal expansion of slavery
    (2) creation of national parks
    (3) distribution of free land to war veterans
    (4) process for territories to become states

4. Which idea guided the development of the Articles of Confederation?

    (1) A strong central government would threaten the rights of the people.
    (2) All the people should be granted the right to vote.
    (3) Most power should rest with the judicial branch.
    (4) Only the central government would have the power to levy taxes.

CHAPTER 6
From Revolution to Statehood

Shays Rebellion

24) **Shays rebellion:** After the revolution, Americans were divided between creditors and debtors. The creditors were those who provided the soldiers with money, food and equipment during the war. The debtors were those that borrowed money and utilized the goods that were provided for the war effort and had no way of repaying their debts. Thus a crisis was brewing and eventually exploded into a full scale rebellion in Massachusetts called Shays Rebellion. It was led by Daniel Shays who attacked the legislature and demanded that all war debts be absolved. Soon the rebellion spawned other rebellions in other states as poor people demanded that their war debts be absolved. The rich, who were in the minority, were extremely upset over these rebellions. However with little military might behind them (since the militia's themselves were part of the rebellion) the states could do very little to stop them.

25) **Reconsidering the Articles of Confederation:** The need for something to be done on a countrywide scale was called for. Congress was called into session. Most legislators came back with the idea of keeping the old Articles of Confederation and adding some enhancements to it. However a small but vocal minority led by the scholarly James Madison had different ideas. They wished to scrap the Articles of Confederation and start again with a new Constitution. This approach was ultimately embraced by congress and a new draft of a Constitution was drawn up.

Federalists V. Anti-Federalists

26) After the new document was drawn up, three fourths of the legislatures (which were 9 out of 13 colonies) were required to ratify it in their own legislatures. In the ensuing months, arguments raged back and forth in the colonies over the merits of the new Constitution. Those against it were called the Anti-Federalists. They argued that despite the fact that it was a modern document etc., it still was highly reminiscent of the dictatorial all powerful government which they just fought to overthrew. They feared that being so powerful, it would trample on the rights of the plain people. Those in favor of the new Constitution were called Federalists. They argued that the system itself would protect the

rights of the plain people by pitting competing centers of powers against each other which would prevent the emergence of any dictatorial powers seen by the old monarchy. Additionally, they argued, ultimately it was in the hands of the people to vote for and elect representative officials to the new government. If they wouldn't like what they stood for, then they could vote them out. Those in favor of the Constitution authored a series of articles which later on became known as the federalist papers which were influential in swaying people to vote in favor of the new constitution. However what really convinced people to support and ratify the constitution was the promise that after the Constitution would be ratified, a bill of rights would be attached to it through the amendment process to allay the concerns of the anti-federalists.

27) In order to ratify the Constitution, there were still three areas that needed to be addressed. They were: the representation of small states v. big states, the status of slaves and the acceptance of tariffs. In order for these issues to be resolved compromises where drafted and agreed upon. Let's examine them.

The Great Compromise

28) The Great Compromise (also known as the Connecticut Compromise): the question arose during the deliberations on the Constitution over what the makeup of the legislatures would be; should they be chosen based on how many people there are in each state, or should they be a set number of delegates to the Congress from every state regardless of its population. If it were to be the first way, then the states with a smaller population would have less representation which would be unfair to the smaller states. If on the other hand it was a set number, then the minority (the small states) would have a greater say compared to the states with larger populations which would be unfair to the larger states. To resolve this issue, a compromise was reached which created a two body legislature-one a House of Representatives which is population based and provides a greater voice to the states with larger numbers of citizens, and a Senate which sets an equal number of delegates for each state.

The 3/5 Compromise

29) The 3/5 compromise: the Southern states argued that slaves should be counted towards the total number of people in a state so that they would have a greater number of delegates. The Northern states argued that this is hypocrisy. They said- since slaves were not treated as equals, then they should not be counted as regular citizens in regards to the census. To resolve this dispute, a compromise was reached whereby every five slaves would be counted as three people in regards to the census for the House of Representatives.

The Commerce Compromise

30) The commerce compromise: the Southern states wanted to abolish the tariff system because they feared retaliatory tariffs from other countries. The Northern states supported the tariff system because it provided an important source of income. The compromise allowed for tariffs to be placed on imports but exports would not be taxed. Eventually 9 states did ratify (or agree to) the new Constitution. Thus the United States of America was formed with a new powerful Constitution.

REGENTS REVIEW

- A bicameral legislature is created in which states have equal representation in the Senate, but representation in the House depends on population. (Aug`12, 8)
- An enslaved person is counted as three-fifths of one person for purposes of both representation and taxation.

1. These two statements describe

    (1) grievances included in the Declaration of Independence
    (2) provisions found in the Articles of Confederation
    (3) compromises reached at the Constitutional Convention
    (4) amendments included in the Bill of Rights

2. Shays' Rebellion (1786) became a concern for many national leaders because it

    (1) indicated there would be future conflicts over the spread of slavery
    (2) exposed fundamental weaknesses in government under the Articles of Confederation
    (3) pointed to the need for federal government regulation of interstate commerce
    (4) showed that frontier settlements were vulnerable to raids by Native American Indians

3. Which statement most accurately explains why the institution of slavery was continued under the original Constitution of the United States?

    (1) The early factory system relied on the labor of slaves.
    (2) The majority of American families owned several slaves.
    (3) Slave rebellions made most whites oppose freedom for African Americans.
    (4) Southern states would not agree to a Constitution that banned slavery

CHAPTER 7
The Constitution: the Legislative Branch

Separation of Powers

31) The Constitution is built on Enlightenment ideas. One of them is Montesquieu's concept of the Separation of powers which states that the best government is one that pits divergent powers against each other. This concept, which lies at the heart of American democracy, is called the Checks and Balance system. Using this idea, the framers divided the government into 3 competing branches. They are the Legislative branch, the Executive branch and the Judicial branch. Let us examine each branch starting with the Legislative branch.

32) The Legislative Branch: The legislative branch is composed of two separate houses which is called a Bicameral Legislature: the House of Representatives and a Senate. The House of Representatives has 435 seats and its makeup is determined by the amount of people in each state. A state with a greater population will have more representatives. The amount of representation a state has in Congress is determined by a census (population count) which, by constitutional mandate, must be performed every ten years to determine the amount of people and hence representatives a state will have. On the other hand the Senate has a total of 100 senators with two coming from each state.

How does the Congress work?

33) The job of Congress is to propose and vote on laws (called bills) for the country. It is the main body that represents the people's interests (popular sovereignty - an idea popularized by Rousseau which was set forth in the preamble of the Constitution - "We the people"…) and is the basis of our democracy. Let us follow the path that a bill takes to become law.

34) A bill is first introduced by any member of Congress; either a member of the House or the Senate. The bill's idea may originate with citizens or by members of the House or Senate. It is given a number by the clerk or presiding officer and then sent to a committee. There are multiple committees in both the House and the Senate. These committees include the rules committee, the finance committee, the security committee, the foreign affairs committee etc. and are made up of powerful members of Congress who get certain seats on various committees usually based on seniority and influence. The bills are sent to the appropriate committees which the bill deals with (security, military, economics, health) etc. In committee, the bills can be done away with if committee members do not take up the bill. This is known as a bill being "pigeonholed". If

the bill is approved with revisions by committee members, the bill can be amended and sent back to the floor to be rewritten with the appropriate recommendation, or just sent with the committee's recommendations to the floor of the house or senate for a vote.

35) It is now sent to the leader of the House or Senate. The speaker of the house or the senate majority leader can kill a bill by not putting it on the agenda. If the bill is allowed to go forward, the bill is given a certain time limit in the house to be debated by both proponents and opponents of the bill. In the senate both opponents and proponents can speak as long as they want. Technically speaking, the opposition in the Senate can create a filibuster which means that the opposition can speak without a time limit until the proponents give up their fight for the bill's passage[1]. The Senate can break a filibuster by bypassing the filibuster if they have 60 out of 100 senators to override their colleagues' objections. After the period of debate is over, the bill is sent to the floor for a vote. If it passes the house by a majority of members (218), then it goes on to the Senate (or vice versa). In the Senate, the bill is voted on and if it passes it goes to the President to get signed. If any of the houses fails to pass the bill then the bill is killed. If the house bill and senate bill are different versions of the same bill, the bills need to be reconciled by a committee of members of both the house and senate. If it is reconciled, then it goes back to both houses and the final reconciled bill is voted on.

36) If the bill is passed by Congress, then it goes on to the President to be signed into law. If the President signs the bill, then it becomes the law of the land. If the President does not like the bill, he can veto it and the bill is killed. If however Congress does not like his veto, it can override it by gathering a 2/3 majority, and then the bill becomes law even without the President's approval.

37) This process shows the concept of checks and balances. It does so by giving the power of the President to kill a bill or the Congress to override his veto.

---

[1] During the 1930s, Senator Huey Long effectively used the filibuster against bills that he thought favored the rich over the poor. The Louisiana senator frustrated his colleagues while entertaining spectators with his recitations of Shakespeare and his reading of recipes for "pot-likkers." Long once held the Senate floor for 15 hours.[5] In 1953, Senator Wayne Morse set a record by filibustering for 22 hours and 26 minutes while protesting the Tidelands Oil legislation. Senator Strom Thurmond broke this record in 1957 by filibustering the Civil Rights Act of 1957 for 24 hours and 18 minutes,[8] although the bill ultimately passed. In 1959, the Senate restored the cloture threshold to two-thirds of those voting

REGENTS REVIEW

1. Which Constitutional principle best protects the public from abuse by one branch of government?

    (1) equality
    (2) federalism
    (3) executive privilege
    (4) checks and balances

2. What is a principle of government that is stated in the Preamble to the United States Constitution?

    (1) Federal laws must be subject to state approval.
    (2) The power of government comes from the people.
    (3) The right to bear arms shall not be infringed.
    (4) All men and women are created equal.

    > "…The accumulation of all powers, legislative, executive, and judiciary, in the same hands, whether of one, a few, or many, and whether hereditary, self-appointed, or elective, may justly be pronounced the very definition of tyranny…."
    > — James Madison

3. Which feature of the United States Constitution was included to address the concern expressed by James Madison?

    (1) electoral college
    (2) checks and balances
    (3) Bill of Rights
    (4) amendment process

CHAPTER 8
The Constitution: The Executive Branch

38) While we have discussed the idea of the President as the legislator who needs to sign his name to federal legislation, he also fills an important part of the government in running the executive branch of government. This branch is one of the three separate but equal branches of government which gives the government a balance of power. Let us discuss its roles in balancing and maintaining governmental stability.

39) **Legislative role:** As we have previously discussed, the President is responsible for either signing legislation into law, or if he wishes, to veto the legislation which would then send the bill back to Congress. We also mentioned that Congress can override his veto and pass legislation over the President's objections.

40) **Commander in Chief:** The President is the head of the army. Included in this job is the responsibility to direct foreign policy. This gives the power to the President to decide whether he wishes to recognize new nations or to negotiate treaties with other countries. If the President negotiates a new treaty, it then needs to be ratified by 2/3 of the senate (another example of checks and balances).

41) **Head of the Federal bureaucracy:** The Federal bureaucracy is in charge in seeing that the laws of the US be faithfully executed. For ex. if Congress passes a law to grant money for highway construction-the bureaucracy is in charge of seeing to it that it gets done. They will hire the contractors (Department of Transportation)-they will oversee that the money is given out (US Treasury), that it is being spent in a proper way and that no laws are being violated in the employment of workers such as discrimination etc. (Justice Department).

42) The job of hiring staff for the Executive Branch is also given to the President. The President makes some 6,000 executive branch appointments before he takes office and some 8,000 after he takes office. (Not that he personally oversees it but that he appoints some of the top posts and they hire others. Thus, he will pick members to run the different departments-transportation secretary, head of the treasury, and the under secretary etc. and they in turn hire the staff). While the President has full authority to hire, the Senate is also granted power in confirming the President's choice. They

give advice and consent by holding hearings about the Presidents top appointee's and then vote on them. Ambassadors are also appointed by the President with the advice and consent of the Senate.

43) The President can direct the Fed. Bureaucracy to take a certain direction which the President decides through something known as executive orders. These orders have the full force of a law under the Constitution (although it doesn't say so explicitly, it is implied and thus understood by the courts) and thus this gives the President much power in choosing how to "faithfully oversee" the laws passed by Congress. For ex. while Congress can allocate money for roads to be built in certain areas, the President can put restrictions on who can build it, how it will be built, when the money will come through etc. However, there is a check on the President's executive order power through the courts which can strike down an executive order as being beyond the Presidential purview (right).

44) Judicial powers: in addition to the power given to the President as stated above, the President is given the authority in the Constitution to appoint Federal Appeals judges and Supreme Court justices. This gives the President power over the courts which serve as a check on the courts power. Besides getting the presidential appointments, these appointees also need to have the Senate's approval and this checks the power of the President to influence the appointments.

45) Part of his power over the courts is the power to grant pardons and reprieves to convicted felons which is usually done at the end of a President's term in office. This is another example of checks and balances in which the president can check the power of the court.

46) Presidents also have a concept known as executive privilege. While not enshrined in the Constitution, it was established after President Washington denied Congress's demands to see Chief Justice John Jay's notes in relation to an unpopular treaty that Washington had made with Britain. He claimed executive privilege to support his right to withhold his notes from Congress. (This is part of what can be described as the unwritten Constitution-parts of American law which are not stated specifically in the Constitution but have nonetheless been accepted though precedent-(tradition of a certain law or practice). For ex. the creation of political parties and a cabinet first established by President Washington are not stated in the constitution but are acknowledged rights.) The Supreme Court has placed limits on this privilege by not allowing it to be used in criminal matters such as when Nixon claimed executive privilege during the Watergate scandal.

47) The President also has the right to withhold information if he feels it can harm national security. For a President to be elected he/she must be must be 35 years old, be born in this country and must be a permanent resident of the USA for at least 14 years. If Congress feels that the President has done something treasonous, they can impeach (throw out) the President. If the President dies in office, the Vice President takes over. In addition to that role, the Vice President acts as the tie breaker in the senate if the Senate is evenly split. While there is no official term limits set out in the Constitution, the unwritten rule was 2 terms established by Washington. This rule was broken by F.D.R who was elected three times and nominated a fourth time but died during his last term in the presidency. After F.D.R's presidency, the 22nd amendment was adopted which barred a President from seeking a third term.

REGENTS REVIEW

1. Which headline illustrates the use of the unwritten Constitution?

    (1) "Washington Establishes a Cabinet"
    (2) "House Votes to Impeach Andrew Johnson"
    (3) "Senate Rejects the Treaty of Versailles"
    (4) "President Nominates John Roberts for Supreme Court (June `12, 7)

2. Which Presidential action is an example of the use of the unwritten Constitution? (Jan, `12, 6)

    (1) holding a cabinet meeting at the White House
    (2) submitting a treaty to the Senate for ratification
    (3) nominating an ambassador to France
    (4) vetoing a bill passed by Congress

3. The establishment of the President's cabinet as part of the United States government was the result of a

    (1) law passed by Congress
    (2) Constitutional amendment
    (3) precedent started by George Washington
    (4) ruling of the United States Supreme Court

CHAPTER 9
The Constitution: the Judicial Branch

48) The function of the judicial branch of government is to rule on cases that hinge on federal law and interpret the Constitution. It is made up of three parts: the Federal Court, the Appeals Court and the Supreme Court. The first court (or federal court) hears and rules on cases/issues which arise from civil disputes that center on federal issues (such as inter-state financial disputes) or criminal issues that arise involving federal issues (for ex. criminal activities that span several states).

49) The second court is the Court of Appeals. This court is referred to if a litigant (one party in a case) is not satisfied with the decision of the first court and wishes to contest the lower court's ruling. This higher court is called the Appeals court and can be found in various geographic zones. If the appeals court upholds the ruling of the lower court, the decision can be appealed to the Supreme Court which may or may not decide to take on the case. Declining to take on the case indicates that the case is over and the appeals court ruling stands. If on the other hand they do take it and rule in favor of the appeals court, then the appeals court stands and the ruling is final. This means that there is virtually no chance of overturning that ruling short of a Presidential pardon or change in law etc.

50) As previously mentioned, the President appoints federal judges who serve a life term. Federal judges are usually rubber stamped by the Senate while the Supreme Court nominees are usually fought over by members of the Senate until a suitable candidate is found.

51) In 1801 an important principle was established by the Supreme Court. John Marshall, the chief justice, who was accused by Jefferson of over stepping his role in what's called Judicial activism, established a principle called Judicial review. Judicial Review refers to the concept that the Supreme Court can review the Constitutionality of the laws made by Congress. This case was established by Marbury vs. Madison[2]. This precedent set in motion an important additional role for the Judicial system in that they also became the final arbiters on the interpretation of the Constitution, and if a law does not meet their standard, that they may strike it down.

---

[2] This case resulted from a petition to the Supreme Court by William Marbury, who had been appointed by President John Adams as Justice of the Peace in the District of Columbia but whose commission was not subsequently delivered. Marbury petitioned the Supreme Court to force Secretary of State James Madison (who did not want the appointments made by John Adams the previous President to go through since Jefferson the new President was his rival) to deliver the documents, but the court, with John Marshall as Chief Justice, denied Marbury's petition, holding that the part of the statute upon which he based his claim, the Judiciary Act of 1789, was unconstitutional. http://en.wikipedia.org/wiki/Marbury_v._Madison and my own notes

We will now examine several other concepts found in the constitution:

- **Federalism:** this means that there is a multi-tiered system of government within our democracy which distributes power among the federal, state and local government and that not all power is invested in the Federal government. For example, the federal government does not control who patrols the street or the highways in NYC or how much those patrolmen get paid. Those issues are left up to the state and local governments. This division of power is at the heart of our democracy and another way that the federal government is prevented from getting too much power. There are some areas where there are shared powers between the Federal gov't and the state and local gov't such as the power to tax.

- **Republican form of Government:** The people vote for members to represent them in office. The way officials are put into office is through the institution of elections. In the House of Representatives, every two years the representatives are put up for reelection. If they win a majority of votes over their opponent then they are elected (or reelected). In the Senate, members are elected every 6 years. A simple majority is all that needs to win a seat in congress. For the Presidency, the Constitution calls for an election every 4 years. However, to win the Presidency one needs to win the majority of votes in the Electoral College. That is, every state is given a certain amount of votes in a body called the Electoral College. In every state that a Presidential candidate wins the majority of the population, all of the electoral votes of that state will go towards that candidate. The winner is the candidate that reaches 270 electoral votes. This means that although a candidate can technically win a majority of the country in numbers of votes (called the popular vote), they will still lose the presidency if his opponent wins the Electoral College such as was the case in Bush V. Gore in the 2000 Presidential race.

- **Constitutionalism-** the basis of how the government acts is dictated by a body of law. This is in contrast to a government which rules capriciously (because they "feel like it") or by the whim of a ruling elite. America is built on the opposite concept; a document(s) and its accompanying body of laws are the basis of how the government will act.

- **Popular Sovereignty**-the basis of the Constitution is that the citizens of the country are in charge of it. There is no ruling elite, (the way it was in every country up to that time) but rather there is a government that is ruled by the people. Thus, if a concept is not mandated by Constitution then it is left to the people to rule.

Bill of Rights

52) The Bill of rights: Despite protests from the federalists that a bill of rights was not necessary, the framers of the Constitution inserted ten amendments to the Constitution to ensure the individual rights of the people. These are the amendments:

First Amendment – Establishment Clause, Free Exercise Clause; freedom of speech, of the press, and of assembly; right to petition

Congress shall make no law respecting an establishment of religion, or prohibiting the free exercise thereof; or abridging the freedom of speech, or of the press; or the right of the people peaceably to assemble, and to petition the Government for a redress of grievances.

Second Amendment – Militia (United States), Sovereign state, Right to keep and bear arms.

A well regulated Militia being necessary to the security of a free State, the right of the people to keep and bear arms shall not be infringed. [5]

Third Amendment – Protection from quartering of troops.

No Soldier shall, in time of peace be quartered in any house, without the consent of the Owner, nor in time of war, but in a manner to be prescribed by law.

Fourth Amendment – Protection from unreasonable search and seizure.

The right of the people to be secure in their persons, houses, papers, and effects, against unreasonable searches and seizures, shall not be violated, and no Warrants shall issue, but upon probable cause, supported by Oath or affirmation, and particularly describing the place to be searched, and the persons or things to be seized.

Fifth Amendment – due process, double jeopardy, self-incrimination, eminent domain.

No person shall be held to answer for any capital, or otherwise infamous crime, unless on a presentment or indictment of a Grand Jury, except in cases arising in the land or naval forces, or in the Militia, when in actual service in time of War or public danger; nor shall any person be subject for the same offence to be twice put in jeopardy of life or limb; nor shall be compelled in any criminal case to be a witness against himself, nor be deprived of life, liberty, or property, without due process of law; nor shall private property be taken for public use, without just compensation.

Sixth Amendment – Trial by jury and rights of the accused; Confrontation Clause, speedy trial, public trial, right to counsel

In all criminal prosecutions, the accused shall enjoy the right to a speedy and public trial, by an impartial jury of the State and district where in the crime shall have been committed, which district shall have been previously ascertained by law, and to be informed of the nature and cause of the accusation; to be confronted with the witnesses against him; to have compulsory process for obtaining witnesses in his favor, and to have the Assistance of Counsel for his defense.

Seventh Amendment – Civil trial by jury.

In suits at common law, where the value in controversy shall exceed twenty dollars, the right of trial by jury shall be preserved, and no fact tried by a jury, shall be otherwise re-examined in any court of the United States, than according to the rules of the common law.

Eighth Amendment – Prohibition of excessive bail and cruel and unusual punishment.

Excessive bail shall not be required, nor excessive fines imposed, nor cruel and unusual punishments inflicted.

Ninth Amendment – Protection of rights not specifically enumerated in the Constitution.

The enumeration in the Constitution, of certain rights, shall not be construed to deny or disparage others retained by the people.

Tenth Amendment – Powers of States and people.

The powers not delegated to the United States by the Constitution, nor prohibited by it to the States, are reserved to the States respectively, or to the people[i].

REGENTS REVIEW

1. Many critics of the Electoral College system point out that it: (Aug '12, 10, 11
   (1) penalizes the states with the smallest population
   (2) encourages the formation of minor political parties
   (3) grants too much influence to the United States Senate
   (4) might not select the candidate with the largest number of popular votes

2. The establishment of judicial review in Marbury v. Madison (1803) gave federal courts the authority to
   (1) decide whether a law is Constitutional
   (2) create lower courts
   (3) approve foreign treaties
   (4) appoint judges to lifetime terms

   Speaker A: As it stands now, the Constitution does not protect civil liberties.

   Speaker B: The system of checks and balances will control any abuse of power by a branch of government.

   Speaker C: The demands of the majority will overwhelm the minority.

   Speaker D: The amendment process will allow the Constitution to be changed when the need arises.

3. How was the concern of Speaker A resolved?
   (1) adoption of the elastic clause
   (2) establishment of the House of Representatives
   (3) creation of the federal court system
   (4) addition of the Bill of Rights (June '12, 4, 5, 8,

4. Which two speakers support the ratification of the Constitution?
   (1) A and D   (3) B and D
   (2) A and C   (4) B and C

5. Judicial review is most accurately described as the power of the
   (1) President to override a decision of the Supreme Court
   (2) state courts to overturn decisions of the Supreme Court
   (3) Senate to approve all Presidential appointments to federal courts
   (4) Supreme Court to determine the Constitutionality of laws

6. Which statement most accurately describes federalism? (Jan '12, 7)

    (1) The judicial branch of government has more power than the other two branches.
    (2) The President and vice President divide executive power.
    (3) Power is divided between the national government and the states.
    (4) Power is shared between the two houses of Congress.

7. Which action is an example of judicial review?

    (1) Congress increased the number of justices on the Supreme Court.
    (2) The Supreme Court declared part of the Judiciary Act of 1789 unConstitutional.
    (3) The Supreme Court heard a case involving a United States ambassador.
    (4) The Chief Justice presided over the impeachment trial of President Andrew Johnson

8. The primary purpose of the Federalist Papers was to

    (1) justify the American Revolution to the colonists
    (2) promote the continuation of British rule
    (3) encourage ratification of the United States Constitution
    (4) support the election of George Washington as President

9. What was a significant effect of Supreme Court decisions under Chief Justice John Marshall (1801–1835)?

    (1) The powers of the federal government were increased.
    (2) The extension of slavery was limited.
    (3) The President's use of the veto power was restricted.
    (4) The states were given more control over interstate commerce.

CHAPTER 10
Post Constitutional America 1791-1820's

53) **Alexander Hamilton:** After the Constitution was ratified, Washington appointed his close advisor Alexander Hamilton as the Secretary of the treasury. As secretary of the treasury, Hamilton established four very important precedents and acts that would set the government on the way towards growth.

a. **The United States needs to repay war debts:** Hamilton felt that it was important for the US government to repay its war debts in order to establish its credit. Additionally he advised that the federal government should assume all the debts of the states, thereby strengthening the power of the federal government over the states.

a. **The establishment of a national bank:** In order to encourage economic growth Hamilton proposed the establishment of a national bank that would lend money and establish financial order after the revolution. To resolve the issue of multiple currencies being used in the country before the war, the US mint was formed at this time to secure a single currency and a single source for all the money in the US. The South opposed the new bank since they had an agricultural economy and didn't need a large bank which they saw as a northern influence over the newly formed government. Additionally, they felt that by attempting to establish a national bank, the federal government was overstepping its constitutional boundaries. However, Hamilton argued that the power given to Congress to establish such a bank was granted by the elastic clause (also see later the strict/loose constructionist debate). This clause states that Congress has the right "To make all Laws which shall be necessary and proper for carrying into Execution the foregoing Powers, and all other Powers vested by this Constitution in the Government of the United States, or in any Department or Officer thereof". Thus, since a national bank was needed for collecting taxes and borrowing funds, Hamilton felt that it was acceptable for Congress to accept it. This precept was challenged in the case of Mculloch vs. Maryland in which Maryland wanted to impose a tax on the 2nd National bank in Maryland because it was an out of state bank. To this, the Supreme Court ruled in favor of the federal government and used Hamilton's argument of the elastic clause, setting the precedent for the expanded role of government.

b. **Argued for the Excise tax:** Hamilton suggested that a tax be imposed on whiskey. Congress accepted the idea and imposed a tax on all whiskey. When cottage producers heard about it, they were incensed and organized a revolt in protest of the tax. The federal government responded by gathering an enormous army of federal troops to the site (larger than any one amount of troops in place during the revolution) which intimidated the rebels and the insurrection ended peacefully. This sent a clear signal to the states that insurrections and rebellions against federal authority would not be tolerated.

a. **The creation of political parties:** members of the administration who were opposed to Hamilton's policies formed a faction or party. The opposition members were called the Democratic-Republicans. In response, Hamilton formed his own political party called the Federalists.

54) Underlying the disagreement between the opposing parties was a philosophical/legal dispute over how to interpret the Constitution. The democratic-republicans favored a strict constructionist approach, which argued that only what the Constitution mandated was to be done and nothing else. This argument was used by Jefferson in his opposition to the establishment of a national bank. The followers of the strict constructionist approach were afraid that the federal government would usurp the states' rights over time by expanding the role and scope of the federal government. Hamilton and the Federalists on the other hand favored a loose constructionist approach which allowed for a more liberal interpretation of the Constitution. They felt that although the constitution clearly spells out the role of the Federal government, its broad and general use of terms allowed for expansion and interpretation.

55) **The Jay treaty or 1795:** the US made a treaty with the British to bring closure to the revolutionary war and better relations between both countries. The Southern states saw this as another attempt to impose the power of the federal government over the States.

56) **Washington's farewell address:** as the term of Washington's presidency came to a close he "warned against foreign influence in domestic affairs and American meddling in European affairs. He warned against bitter partisanship in domestic politics and called for men to move beyond partisanship and serve the common good. He warned against "permanent alliances with any portion of the foreign world", saying the United States must concentrate primarily on American interests. He counseled friendship and commerce with all nations, but warned against involvement in European wars and entering into long-term "entangling" alliances. The address quickly set American values regarding foreign affairs[ii]"

The War of 1812

57) **The war of 1812:** despite the Jay treaty which was supposed to relax the tensions between the US and Britain, it was not long before war flared once again.

The cause for the war was fourfold:

- **Impressments:** the British were capturing sailors who had deserted their navy and joined the more lucrative American merchant ships. The British would seize American ships and induct deserters and others into their naval service.

- **Trade disputes:** The US supported Napoleon with friendly commercial relations. Being that the British were at war with the French, and had imposed trade restrictions upon them, the support served as a source of contention between the two countries.

- **The British still controlled the Northwest Territory** and wished to hold onto it. The US wished to expand into that area.

- **The US wished to stop the raids by Indian groups** from the Northwest Territory whom the British were supplying with arms and helping in their attacks on the US.

58) **The outcome of the war:** although the US emerged as victors in the war, little changed for the two countries in terms of territory. In addition, by the time the war was over, Napoleons reign had come to an end making the issue of trading with England's enemy irrelevant. The end of the war did however usher in an era of peaceful relations between the two countries through the 19th and 20th centuries.

59) **Monroe Doctrine:** the doctrine put forth by President James Monroe stated that the Western hemisphere was off limits to further colonization. Furthermore, any attempt at any further colonization by western powers would be seen by the US as an attack on its sovereignty.

REGENTS REVIEW

> ...Europe has a set of primary interests which to us have none or a very remote relation. Hence she must be engaged in frequent controversies, the causes of which are essentially foreign to our concerns. Hence, therefore, it must be unwise in us to implicate [connect] ourselves by artificial ties in the ordinary vicissitudes [changes] of her politics or the ordinary combinations and collisions of her friendships or enmities [antagonisms]....
> — President George Washington, Farewell Address, 1796

1. According to the passage, President Washington believed that the United States should

    (1) seek financial aid from European nations
    (2) end all existing European friendships
    (3) avoid involvement in the political disputes of Europe
    (4) discontinue commercial relations with Europe (Aug. `12, 9

2. A strict interpretation versus a loose interpretation of the Constitution was most evident in the debate over the

    (1) creation of the Bank of the United States in 1791
    (2) decision to declare war on Great Britain in 1812
    (3) annexation of Florida in 1821
    (4) issuance of the Monroe Doctrine in 1823

3. On the issue of creating a national bank, Secretary of State Thomas Jefferson and Secretary of the Treasury Alexander Hamilton differed on whether to

    (1) apply a strict or loose interpretation of the Constitution
    (2) establish a tariff to raise revenue
    (3) use deposits to finance a new navy
    (4) issue loans to farmers (Jan `12, 8,11, 12)

4. The outcome of the Whiskey Rebellion (1794) strengthened the authority of the

    (1) national government
    (2) state governors
    (3) territorial legislatures
    (4) local police

5. The War of 1812 has been called the "Second War for American Independence" primarily because the

   (1) British blocked United States access to the port of New Orleans
   (2) United States continued to resist taxes imposed by Great Britain
   (3) British government had never fully respected the United States as a free nation
   (4) United States and Great Britain had not signed a peace treaty after the Revolutionary War

6. Alexander Hamilton's proposal to create a national bank and Thomas Jefferson's proposal to purchase the Louisiana Territory were criticized because both actions would

   (1) place too much power in the hands of Congress
   (2) violate protections in the Bill of Rights
   (3) increase foreign influence in the United States
   (4) require a loose interpretation of the Constitution

7. The main purpose of the Monroe Doctrine (1823) was to

   (1) stake a claim to Mexican territory
   (2) limit European influence in the Americas
   (3) force the British out of the Oregon Territory
   (4) establish full control over Canada

8. The elastic clause of the United States Constitution gives Congress the power to

   (1) "make rules for the government and regulation of the land and naval forces;…"
   (2) "regulate commerce with foreign nations, and among the several states, and with the Indian tribes;…"
   (3) "lay and collect taxes, duties, imports and excises,…"
   (4) "make all laws which shall be necessary and proper for carrying into execution the foregoing powers,…"

9. During the 1830s, the development of a national two-party political system was mainly the result of

   (1) conflicts over the use of the Monroe Doctrine
   (2) debates over the National Bank and tariffs
   (3) disputes over the Oregon boundary
   (4) controversy over the Indian Removal Act

CHAPTER 11
America: 1810-1830

The American System

60) The American system: the American system, promoted by Senator Henry Clay, was a multi-faceted approach to strengthen American industry. It followed Hamilton's approach of expanded government, and promoted Tariffs (taxes) as a way in which to protect the US's developing industries from British goods. It also argued for raising taxes in order to develop infrastructure to unify the country through railroads and roads. Thus a major expansion of the nation's infrastructure was implemented. It was also at this time that Canals were dug such as the Erie Canal connecting Lake Erie of the Great Lakes and the Hudson River. The Canal had a large impact on trade between the east and west coast by providing a faster and cheaper way to transport farm goods to the east coast. In addition, the canal facilitated the migration of Americans to the west.

61) Sectionalism: Despite the unity achieved through the building of roads which made migration and transportation easier, the South and the North remained divided over the use of tariffs. Furthermore, the South and North were growing more and more divided over the slavery issue. Thus, while a sense of connectedness was growing, it also seemed that parts of the country were experiencing a great deal of tension and divisiveness. This trend was called sectionalism.

62) Immigration: beginning in the 1830's and onwards, mass immigration began to the US from Central and Western Europe. The majority of these migrants were from Ireland, Germany, Italy and other European countries. Many were seeking political stability, such as the refugees from Germany who were fleeing revolutions, while others were seeking economic benefits such as those fleeing Ireland. In particular, a potato famine struck Ireland in 1845 and many Irish, facing the prospects of starvation and death, fled their country for the US. Many German Jews, sensing economic opportunity, immigrated to the US and participated in the settlement of the frontier as peddlers, prospectors and miners. Other immigrants helped American industrialization as they filled jobs in American factories.

63) Slavery: in the south, slavery was in full force with cotton being the main crop on which the slaves worked. Slaves at times rebelled against their overlords such as the revolt at Harpers Ferry but were always repulsed by their masters.

64) Election of Andrew Jackson: with the election of Andrew Jackson, the process of how presidents were chosen changed. Until this time, presidents were elected based on their party's nomination. However with the election of Andrew Jackson, the president was elected by popular appeal. Jackson, a war hero, won the approval of the majority of the people and won the election. Upon assuming office, Jackson appointed his cronies into positions of leadership which was termed the spoils system. Jackson's justification for this was his desire to remove entrenched bureaucrats.

65) The Nullification crisis of 1828: During Jackson's presidency, congress issued a protective tariff on goods coming into the US. This tax would help protect fledgling US industries against the competition of lower priced goods produced in foreign countries. The South vehemently opposed the tariff, calling it the Tariff of Abominations. They claimed that while the tariff would benefit Northern industries, the South, a mostly agricultural society, would be forced to pay higher prices for certain foreign goods for which they depended on. They also feared that the tariff would also interfere with trade arrangements that they shared with Britain. After congress passed the tariff over the objections of the southern states, South Carolina, with the support of Jackson's vice president John C. Calhoun, declared that the tariff was null and void in their state. Both sides began to prepare for war, but backed down at the end after both sides negotiated a quiet change in the tariff that spared bloodshed. This crisis, despite being peaceably resolved, bared the uncomfortable truth of sectionalism in the country.

66) Indian removal: Jackson advocated for the removal of all American Indians from the eastern side of the Mississippi. Many Indians were forced by gunpoint to leave their ancestral lands and go west. This trail that they forged in their migration was termed the trail of tears. When the Cherokee nation won a case in the Supreme Court against the policy of Indian removal in Worcester vs. Georgia, President Jackson ignored the opinion of the court and refused to uphold the law.

67) Louisiana Purchase and the westward movement: In 1803 Thomas Jefferson bought the territory of Louisiana from the French for 15 million dollars doubling the size of the US territory. In addition to attaining the goal of expanding the US empire, the US also gained control of the Great Plains and the Port of New Orleans, a strategic area for trade and commerce, in the newly purchased area. Many Americans went to the west and settled there. This westward migration was also partially spurred on by the concept of manifest destiny, or the belief that it was the divine mission of the US to expand its borders over the land in order to spread the ideals of democracy.

REGENTS REVIEW

1. A major reason for purchasing the Louisiana Territory (1803) was to
    (1) gain access to the Ohio Territory
    (2) remove the British from the borders of the United States
    (3) secure control of the port of New Orleans
    (4) open the Rocky Mountains to miners (Aug. '12, 12)

2. President Andrew Jackson used the spoils system to
    (1) attack the Tariff of Abominations
    (2) reward supporters with United States government jobs
    (3) win support for construction of the Erie Canal
    (4) gain passage of the Indian Removal Act (June '12, 10, 11)

3. The majority of immigrants who arrived in the United States between 1800 and 1860 came from
    (1) East Asia
    (2) Latin America
    (3) northern and western Europe
    (4) southern and eastern Europe

4. The Erie Canal contributed to the development of the United States by
    (1) eliminating the need for railroads
    (2) linking the Great Lakes to the Atlantic Coast
    (3) becoming the major trade route to California
    (4) allowing southern planters to ship their cotton westward

5. Which Supreme Court decision is most closely associated with the Trail of Tears?
    (1) McCulloch v. Maryland (1819)
    (2) Gibbons v. Ogden (1824)
    (3) Worcester v. Georgia (1832)
    (4) Dred Scott v. Sanford (1857)

6. Which geographic area was added to the United States by the Louisiana Purchase?
    (1) Appalachian Mountains
    (2) Columbia River valley
    (3) Great Plains
    (4) Piedmont Plateau

7. How did completion of the Erie Canal in 1825 affect United States commerce?
    (1) New York City lost business as manufacturing centers grew in the West.
    (2) United States exports to European countries declined.
    (3) Western farmers gained better access to East Coast markets.
    (4) The Midwest became the center of textile production.

CHAPTER 12
Reform, Growth and Conflict: America 1830's-1860's

Reform movements of the 1800's

68) Reform movements of the 1800's:

a. **Abolitionist movement:** the movement to free slaves. Abolitionists conducted meetings and published newspapers to draw attention to the plight of the slaves and demand their freedom. Harriet Tubman, a former slave became famous for her role in helping slaves escape through the Underground Railroad, a secret route which slaves could follow up north to freedom.

a. **Women's rights:** women such as Elizabeth Cady Stanton, Lucreita Mott, and Susan B. Anthony pushed for universal suffrage in which women would be given the right to vote as well as other legal rights, such as the right to own property etc. While they didn't see immediate results, over time the campaign was successful and women achieved the right to vote along with other rights previously denied to women. This movement began at the Seneca Falls convention in upstate NY in 1848.

a. **The movement for public education:** reformers such as Horace Mann saw the need for public education if the country were to progress. In 1837, Horace Mann, who came from Massachusetts, became secretary of that state's board of education. He reformed the school system by increasing state spending on schools and lengthened the school year. Moreover, he divided students into grades, and introducing standardized textbooks which helped students achieve a better education. Many schools in the North followed Mann's ideas while in the South, little progress was made in this area partially due to the fact that they cared little for progressive reforms.

b. **Mental hospitals:** up until that time, mental hospitals were nightmarish places filled with patients living in horrid conditions. U.S. reformer Dorothea Dix observed that mentally ill people in Massachusetts, both men and women and all ages, were incarcerated with criminals, left unclothed in darkness and without heat or bathrooms. Many were chained and beaten. Over the next 40 years, Dix lobbied to establish 32 state hospitals for the mentally ill[iii].

a. **Temperance movement:** This movement, which was dominated by women, wanted to ban the consumption of alcoholic drinks in the effort to eliminate the problem of drunkenness in society. Eventually, the constitution was amended in 1919 to include Prohibition, which prohibited the manufacture and sale of alcoholic beverages (except for religious purposes). After a few years it was seen as a failure, as criminal elements began large enterprises of its sale, and people in general ignored the law. This led to a constitutional repeal a couple of years later in 1933.

Expansion

69) Expansion: during the mid-1800's, the US grew to encompass all of the states on the mainland. This included the acquisition of Texas, California, and New Mexico during the Mexican-American war of 1846-8 which ended with the Treaty of Guadalupe Hidalgo. The underlying cause for the war was the desire for conquest and Manifest Destiny, but actually started after an unprovoked attack by Spanish troops against American troops near the banks of the Rio Grande. Seeing his opportunity to expand the US, President Polk used the context of the attack to go to war with Mexico. Once these states were acquired, people quickly moved and settled there, especially after gold was found in California in the late 1840's (called the Gold rush).

70) Sectionalism again: the battle over slavery began to heat up during this reform period. The Dread Scott case tested the issue of slavery when a white master moved from a slave state to non-slave state and back, and wished to hold on to his slave. The Supreme Court ruled that slaves are property and therefore not given any rights.

71) Legal precedents were used in both sides of the debate over slavery. Those in opposition to slavery pointed to laws such as the Northwest Ordinance of 1787 which prohibited slavery in the Northwest Territory, while the South claimed the 3/5th compromise as proof that the authors of the constitution accepted the concept of slavery.

72) The big issue was how to resolve the status of slavery in the new states. Many solutions were attempted. In 1820 the Missouri Compromise suggested that the US be split in half and that any state below Missouri would be a slave state and all those that were above it were to be free states. In other attempts at compromise, the Compromise of 1850 was established which called for the return of all runaway slaves in exchange for California being admitted into the Union as a free state. In 1854 the Kansas Nebraska Act gave the new states of Kansas and Nebraska the ability to decide for themselves (Popular sovereignty) if they wanted slavery. When the states began to choose, members of both sides of the debate entered into the territory hoping to swing the vote in their favor. As the debates got heated both sides engaged in acts of violence against each other and this compromise subsequently was renamed the Bleeding Compromise. In 1860 Abraham Lincoln, who ran on an anti-slavery platform, ran against Senator Douglas and had a series of highly publicized debates called the Lincoln-Douglas debates. The South threatened that if Lincoln won they would secede (break away) from the Union. A last ditch effort was made to stop the crisis with a proposal that would extend the Missouri compromise across the land. The compromise failed, Lincoln won and the South seceded. President Buchanan whose term was about to conclude and did not

want to deal with the matter of secession, waited out the matter and let Lincoln deal with it himself.

73) When Lincoln was elected President, he declared secession not an option and the Civil War broke out. It was a bloody war with over 600,000 casualties. The most killed in any one battle was at Gettysburg, and where Lincoln later gave the famous address - the Gettysburg address. In this address, he discussed the moral issues raised by slavery. In 1863 he declared the Emancipation Proclamation whereby he freed all the slaves and which led to many African American regiments serving in the Union army. Eventually this led to the 13, 14 and 15 amendments to be passed in which slavery was outlawed (13th), all peoples born in the US are called citizens and punishments outlined for the South (14th) and that all citizens have the right to vote (15th). During the war Lincoln acted in a constitutionally controversial manner by prohibiting certain forms of speech (due to the sensitivity of the time) and suspending Habeas Corpus. Thus, members in border states who advocated for war, were arrested and their rights were curtailed. Eventually the bloody war came to a close with a victory for the North. However for Lincoln the victory was short lived after Lincoln was shot and killed by a southern sympathizer after the war.

REGENTS REVIEW

1. **In the 1840s, President James K. Polk's belief in Manifest Destiny led to**
   (1) a war with Mexico
   (2) an alliance with several South American nations
   (3) the establishment of new colonies in the Caribbean
   (4) a ban on the activities of northern abolitionists (Aug. `12, 13, 14, 16, 30)

2. **The principle of popular sovereignty was an important part of the**
   (1) Indian Removal Act   (3) Homestead Act
   (2) Kansas-Nebraska Act   (4) Dawes Act

3. **A primary reason for the passage of the 14th amendment in 1868 was to**
   (1) prohibit the secession of states
   (2) uphold the legality of the Black Codes
   (3) continue the Presidential plan for Reconstruction
   (4) guarantee citizenship rights to the newly freed slaves

4. **Which factor contributed most to the repeal of national Prohibition in 1933?**
   (1) the inability of government to enforce the law
   (2) an improvement in the economy
   (3) a decline in organized crime
   (4) the start of World War II

5. **Before the start of the Civil War, many Southern political leaders supported**
   (1) States rights   (3) voting rights for women
   (2) higher tariff rates   (4) repeal of the Fugitive Slave Act (June `12, 12, 13)

   > …With malice toward none; with charity for all; with firmness in the right, as God gives us to see the right, let us strive on to finish the work we are in; to bind up the nation's wounds; to care for him who shall have borne the battle, and for his widow, and his orphan—to do all which may achieve and cherish a just, and a lasting peace, among ourselves, and with all nations.
   >   — President Abraham Lincoln, 1865

6. **This statement by President Lincoln contributed to disagreements over the**
   (1) continuation of a military draft
   (2) provision of free land to settlers
   (3) negotiations with foreign nations after the Civil War
   (4) treatment of the former Confederate states and their leaders

"...Our whole system of self-government will crumble either if officials elect what laws they will enforce or citizens elect what laws they will support. The worst evil of disregard for some law is that it destroys respect for all law...." (June `12, 26)
— President Herbert Hoover, 1929

7. Which issue is President Hoover discussing in this statement?
   (1) national Prohibition
   (2) environmental conservation
   (3) Social Security taxes
   (4) voting rights for women

8. Which heading best completes the partial outline below? (Jan, `12, 14)
   I. _____
   A. Suspension of habeas corpus
   B. Signing of Emancipation Proclamation
   C. Election of President Lincoln to second term
   (1) Wartime Propaganda Campaigns
   (2) Limits on Civil Liberties During Wartime
   (3) Decreased Rights of Minorities
   (4) Events During the Civil War

"Missouri Compromise Allows Two New States Into the Union"
"Congress Agrees to Compromise of 1850"
"Popular Sovereignty Adopted Under Kansas-Nebraska Act"

9. Which issue is reflected in these headlines?
   (1) status of slavery in the territories and states
   (2) growth of agriculture on the Great Plains
   (3) clash of federal and state powers
   (4) conflicts with foreign nations over the West

10. What was a major result of the Civil War?
    (1) The judiciary became the dominant branch of the federal government.
    (2) Congress passed an amendment to provide for the direct election of senators.
    (3) The power of the central government was strengthened.
    (4) States were given the right to secede from the Union.

11. The repeal of national Prohibition in 1933 showed that
    (1) alcohol consumption was not socially acceptable
    (2) the government should lower the drinking age
    (3) crime rates had fallen to record low levels
    (4) unpopular laws are difficult to enforce

CHAPTER 13
Reconstruction (1865-1877)

74) After the war concluded, with slavery gone, and the South in shambles, great divisions arose between members of Lincoln's party over how to reconstruct the South. Many members harbored great resentment over the fact that the South caused so much bloodshed and wanted to see the South punished. On the other hand Lincoln and other like-minded members wanted to see the South reconstructed speedily with little to no punishments for the South.

75) While Congress debated the future of Reconstruction, General Sherman, a union general who had conquered Savanna, Georgia, gave a special order which gave all emancipated slaves 40 acres and a mule. As the concept of African Americans owning land formerly owned by white planters began to seep into their consciousness, white Southerners fought back by instituting the Black Codes that would keep African Americans near conditions of slavery. These codes forced African Americans to work only as farmhands and also allowed the "selling" of non-working African Americans as slaves again. Additionally, President Andrew Johnson (who was not very supportive towards the freedom of African Americans) pardoned thousands of white planters and reversed the earlier policy of Sherman's black land ownership. With this, many abandoned fields were given back to the original white owners. This policy was instituted because both Northern and Southern whites began to fear that African American farmers would no longer work and that the whole Southern cotton economy would die out. Now that they were pushed off of the fields given to them by General Sherman, sharecropping, in which farmers rent out a field for a portion of the crops, and other forms of farm work were taken up by African American farmers.

76) Meanwhile, most whites agreed with the moderate republicans that only limited rights be given to African Americans. However many republicans were dismayed by the results of President Johnsons lenient policies which led to massacres of Black freedmen, and were shocked at the brutality of the Black codes which denied the African Americans many basic rights. Many republicans were radicalized (and given the name Radical republicans) and felt that the South needed to be treated more harshly and successfully pushed through the passage of Radical Reconstruction. It banned (with a Constitutional amendment) the right for former confederate leaders to remain in power, divided up the South into 5 military districts, and demanded that new state Constitution's in the South be drawn up and have Congressional approval.

77) As soon as new legislatures began to form, African Americans began to fill positions of power at the state level. However this served to increase the animosity of Southern whites towards the African Americans especially as they saw their former slaves occupying governmental positions previously held by them. In addition, they resented the Union troops who had settled in the South to help in the military arrangements that came with radical reconstruction. The white southern press resorted to pejorative names for these people calling them Carpetbaggers, after their small bags they carried with them, and the white southerners who supported the reconstruction were labeled Scalawags.

78) Seeing that government was against them, some whites began resorting to violence in an effort to keep African Americans out of power and from voting. Secret societies such as the Ku Klux Klan, the White League and the Red Shirts organized to keep African Americans in their place as subordinate and whites in positions of power. African Americans, republicans and northerners were all targeted with beatings, lynching's (death by a mob) and other forms of intimidation. When the federal government intervened in the South to protect the African Americans, the government lost a lot of its support for reconstruction among the white Southerners.

79) In addition to the white violence taking its toll on African American voters, most southerners where deeply dissatisfied with the Radical reconstruction program and threw their support behind the Democratic Party. Eventually, the South turned solidly democratic and was termed the solid South.

80) The next President after Johnson was the celebrated Union war hero General Ulysses S. Grant. Many scandals occurred during his presidency, such as the whiskey ring scandal in which officials in Grant's administration were found to be accepting bribes, and the credit mobilier scandal in which members of congress where bribed not to investigate corruption. During these years, the Republican Party also suffered from internal divisions and the president was blamed for an economic depression in 1873. These scandals and problems further contributed to the weakening of public support for the Republican party.

81) In the next election, the republican candidate Rutherford B Hayes won a very narrow victory. In 1877, seeing the country on the verge of another crises, a compromise was struck (called the compromise of 1877) in which the President agreed to end reconstruction if the South accepted him as President. Thus ended the Reconstruction era.

Segregation

82) Once reconstruction was over, White southerners instituted a series of laws aimed at keeping African Americans and whites segregated (separated) known as the Jim Crow laws. Stories which glorified the slavery period known as the Antebellum (existing before the war) South spread at the time and which served to justify support for the Jim Crow laws. To keep African Americans from gaining political power, whites in the South began to institute poll laws. For ex. some states instituted a poll tax which demanded that potential voters pay before voting. This law would essentially prevent the poor African American population from voting. Other states created literacy tests which demanded that only people who could read could vote. Being that African Americans had little schooling, very few could pass the tests which would allow them to

vote. If these laws presented a problem for poor or uneducated whites, southern states instituted the grandfather clause which allowed one to vote if their grandfather had the right to vote.

83) African Americans fought the segregation laws by going to the courts and arguing that segregation was unconstitutional being that it treated African Americans unfairly. The Supreme Court however rejected their argument and ruled in Plessy vs. Ferguson (in 1896) that separate but equal is equal. Thus, segregation was upheld by the highest court in the land. (for more on this case see #169)

84) After losing in the courts, African Americans looked for different solutions to deal with the new reality. Booker T. Washington argued that African Americans should seek economic improvement and thereby attain the respect of the whites which would end segregation. WEB Dubois argued that African Americans should earn a liberal arts education and then demand that they be treated as equals. Others (such as Marcus Garvey) countered that the white Americans will never respect African Americans and suggested that freedmen go back to Africa.

REGENTS REVIEW

1. After the Civil War, white Southern landowners used sharecropping to
    (1) set up schools to educate formerly enslaved persons
    (2) encourage freedmen to migrate north
    (3) maintain a cheap labor supply
    (4) sell their plantations to formerly enslaved persons (Aug. '12, 17, 20)

2. The Supreme Court decision in Plessy v. Ferguson (1896) affected African Americans by
    (1) granting voting rights
    (2) expanding civil rights
    (3) upholding racial segregation
    (4) guaranteeing equal wages

3. After the Civil War, the sharecropping system emerged in the South primarily as a way to
    (1) diversify agricultural production
    (2) provide a labor supply to plantation owners
    (3) give forty acres of land to freedmen
    (4) guarantee economic equality for African Americans (June '12, 14, 16)

4. Starting in the 1870s, Jim Crow laws were enacted in Southern states as a means to
    (1) provide an education for formerly enslaved persons
    (2) protect the voting rights of formerly enslaved persons
    (3) enforce racial segregation
    (4) ensure equal protection under the law

5. Jim Crow laws passed in the South during the late 1800s were designed to (Jan '12, 15)
    (1) support civil rights for African Americans
    (2) create a system of legal segregation
    (3) give free land to formerly enslaved persons
    (4) compensate landowners for damage done during the Civil War

6. What was a result of the disputed Presidential election of 1876?
    (1) Reconstruction ended as federal troops were removed from the South.
    (2) Slavery was reestablished in the South by state legislatures.
    (3) New state laws were passed in the South to guarantee equal rights for African Americans.
    (4) A Constitutional amendment was adopted to correct problems with the electoral college system.

7. The Supreme Court decision in the case of Plessy v. Ferguson (1896) affected civil rights in the United States by

    (1) ruling that segregated public schools were unconstitutional
    (2) rejecting the legal basis of Jim Crow laws
    (3) approving racial segregation in public facilities
    (4) strengthening the protections of the 14th Amendment

8. Which argument was used by President Abraham Lincoln to explain his policy of leniency toward the South after the Civil War?

    (1) Most Southerners have remained loyal to the Union during the war.
    (2) Most Southerners are willing to grant equality to formerly enslaved persons.
    (3) The federal government has no authority to punish states for secession.
    (4) Healing the nation's wounds quickly is essential.

9. In the Compromise of 1877 that ended Reconstruction, Republicans agreed to

    (1) withdraw federal troops from the South
    (2) support the Black Codes
    (3) award the presidency to Democrat Samuel Tilden
    (4) accept the Supreme Court decision in *Dred Scott v. Sanford*

10. Literacy tests and grandfather clauses were enacted in the South after the Reconstruction Era primarily to

    (1) increase the number of women voters
    (2) limit the number of African American voters
    (3) guarantee that voters could read and write
    (4) ensure that formerly enslaved persons met property requirements

CHAPTER 14
The Growth of American Business 1880-1920

85) After the Civil War, the South's economy was devastated. Plantations were overrun, fields destroyed, and crops ruined. This provided an opportunity to change the basic underlying structure of the economy and industrialize. Factories and other advancements in technology began to infiltrate into the South, as they moved to catch up with the rest of the industrialized world.

86) While this was happening in the South, the North was moving ahead economically as well. New business forms began to take shape. The corporation was formed which divided up a company among many shareholders, increasing capital flow (money invested) in a company. It also reduced the risk on the Entrepreneurs (people who start a business) who started companies with the hope of building a fortune. Also, during this time, the US government encouraged people to settle the West beginning with a series of laws in 1862 and continuing until 1976. These laws, called the Homestead Acts, granted people land virtually for nothing, on condition that they stay and settle the land for 5 years.

87) While some of these developments in the world of finance were good for the economy, others had negative effects. Monopolies, or large businesses which controlled entire markets and industries, began to spring up. These monopolies stifled competition leading to high prices, shoddy service, and a lack of opportunity for others. Other monopolies developed in which several major businesses would agree with each other not to compete by dividing up areas of business and fixing prices. This is called a Pool. Trusts were also created in which many corporations agreed to have one board make decisions for them, and in return, would receive a share of the profits. Conglomerates, a legal form of business in which one company with a lot of market power and capital would own various unrelated businesses, also began during this period. When trusts were outlawed, holding companies were formed (where a company owns the stock of another company) to circumvent this specific outlawed practice.

88) As these new business grew, the entrepreneurs that began these companies acquired great wealth. People such as Andrew Carnegie, John D. Rockefeller, and Andrew Mellon all became fabulously wealthy, building fortunes that were amongst the greatest in the world. These wealthy

individuals flaunted their wealth, building for themselves fabulous homes and living highly ostentatious lifestyles in what became known as conspicuous consumption. This public display of wealth brought them a shower of criticism from the public who accused them of being robber barons who became wealthy on the backs of poor laborers. In response to the criticism, many of these wealthy individuals began to give away lots of their money in great acts of philanthropy, or public charitable giving, in order to ameliorate the publics anger. Carnegie supported the building of public libraries. Rockefeller gave money to many colleges and Mellon supported the arts and other research causes.

89) The basic economic principle on which the US economy operated then was the Free Enterprise System. This system, which is at the heart of capitalism, says that people are free to do what they need to in order to help themselves earn a living. It also promotes the concept of Laissez-faire which argues that government should take a "hands off" approach to affairs of the economy. While this system greatly enhanced the profits of the few who built themselves business empires, the vast majority of the factory workers saw very little economic benefit from this system. Advocates for this unequal economic state of affairs justified the inequality on Social Darwinism which theorized that economic inequality was a product of selective breeding that allowed those who were most "fit" to rise to the top. Therefore, they argued, it would be "unnatural" for the government to intervene.

90) During the 1880's, while little change occurred in the free enterprise system, the country took some symbolic steps to change the status quo by passing laws that would, in theory, put constraints on the free market system. The first step was the Interstate Commerce act of 1887 which attempted to regulate the railroads and to stop their pools. In 1890 the government bowed to public pressure and passed the Sherman Antitrust Act which, while in practice was largely ignored until President Theodore Roosevelt (1901-1909), was important in laying the groundwork for government regulation of the economy. This law required the federal government to investigate and pursue those that were suspected of violating the act.

91) While the government only took small steps to rectify the economic imbalances during the late 1800's, action was taken by ordinary workers to ease their problems of poor pay and poor working conditions. Workers organized into labor unions such as the AFL (American Federation of Labor which took in skilled workers) and the women's International Ladies Garment Workers Union (ILGWU) and used collective bargaining (group demands with the threat of a strike) in hope of achieving their demands for higher wages and better working conditions. Some notable (though unsuccessful) strikes were the Great Railway strike of 1877, the Haymarket strike of 1886 (which saw much violence and which turned the public against unions), the Homestead strike of 1892, the Pullman strike of 1894 and the Lawrence textile strike of 1912 (which was successful). At first, unions were viewed the by public as being composed of anarchists, anti-industrialists, or as socialists. Over time though, their reputation improved as the unions true values and goals became known.

REGENTS REVIEW

1. In the late 1800s, the term robber baron was used to describe some owners of big businesses primarily because they
   (1) favored free trade
   (2) eliminated competition using ruthless methods
   (3) opposed the formation of corporations
   (4) provided workers with high wages

2. During the late 1800s, which development led to the other three?
   (1) formation of labor unions
   (2) increased demand for natural resources
   (3) federal regulation of business trusts
   (4) growth of industry

3. In the late 19th and early 20th centuries, a major goal of the American Federation of Labor (AFL) was to
   (1) end restrictions on child labor
   (2) admit women to the industrial workforce
   (3) improve wages and working conditions
   (4) join all workers into a single union

4. During the late 1800s, the idea of Social Darwinism was used to explain the
   (1) development of the Granger movement
   (2) need for settlement homes
   (3) creation of a national parks system
   (4) success or failure of businesses

5. One reason the American Federation of Labor (AFL) was successful was that this organization
   (1) focused on the needs of skilled workers
   (2) rejected the use of strikes and boycotts
   (3) ended the use of blacklists by employers
   (4) called for government ownership of industry

6. The formation of national labor unions in the late 1800s was mainly a response to
   (1) passage of federal laws that favored workers
   (2) laws restricting immigration and naturalization
   (3) poor working conditions and low wages in many industries
   (4) economic depressions that had led to high unemployment

CHAPTER 15
Urbanization and Immigration: 1880's-1920's

92) As the late 1800's dawned, millions of immigrants were drawn by America's promise of a better economic and political life. Religious freedom, and a guarantee of greater economic and political security brought millions of Russians and Eastern Europeans to these shores.

Urbanization

93) The immigrants gathered in large cities. Cities swelled as people sought employment which was abundant in cities. High rise buildings, called Tenements, squeezed one next to another, arose to house these new immigrants. The squalor, overcrowding, and unhygienic practices of the times led to periodic outbreaks of diseases such as cholera and tuberculosis, spreading rapidly in such close living quarters. Additionally, big cities fed a culture of corruption. Politicians, seizing on immigrants' desire for employment, promised jobs and favors to new immigrants in return for their votes.

94) Advantages of the city: However, living in the cities had its advantages as well. Large numbers of people were able to enjoy the arts and parks that the cities offered. Large public museums, dedicated by wealthy philanthropists, expanded the horizons of young and old alike. Finally, it was in the cities that the greatest innovations were found, such as electricity, street lamps, cars, etc.

95) Class structure in the city: In many American cities, society was divided according to class. There was the working (or the poor class as they were referred to) class, the middle class (professionals etc.), and the upper class. In cities like NYC, neighborhoods were divided along class lines.

96) Role of women: As America industrialized, the role of women began to change. Due to low wages given to workers, many women were forced to work in factories to help the family survive. In doing so, the status of women began to change slowly from homemakers and small shop owners to breadwinners and members of the workforce. This emboldened many women to advocate for more rights and privileges.

Nativism

97) Nativism: As new immigrants came to America from Asia, and Eastern and Southern Europe, an anti-immigrant sentiment arose in

America. Nativism, as it was called, was a movement which painted all new immigrants as foreign invaders who would take away jobs from Americans and negatively impact American culture. It argued that the new immigrants were illiterate, uncouth, and poor and therefore not eligible for citizenship. This movement eventually led to legislation that slowed down immigration in the late 1800's such as the Chinese Exclusion Act of 1882. Additionally, the Gentleman's Agreement in 1907 was an agreement between the US and Japan which sought to end immigration by stopping the issuance of passports for potential emigres from Japan. Both these moves slowed down immigration from Asia, and later led to an almost complete stop in the 1920's.

98) **Attitudes towards immigration:** Historically, there have been three general attitudes towards immigration in the US. At first people argued that new immigrants should try to assimilate into the new country. This approach argues that all new immigrants should seek to lose their habits and characteristics from the "old country" and adapt the new language and culture of the US. Over time this attitude began to fade as the country became more diverse and a new attitude, the melting pot theory, became popular. This theory argues that immigrants should preserve some vestiges of their old country and culture while adopting to the new culture of America. Using this approach would help add to American culture and diversity, while blending new immigrants together into one new unified type. The latest attitude on immigration has been the multicultural theory. This theory reasons that people who come to the new country do not need to leave any of their old habits that they held in the old country or try and blend into the majority culture. Instead each culture should retain their authentic culture without feeling pressure to bend to the majority's culture.

Indian Wars

99) Indian Wars: Beginning with their arrival at the start of the 16th century, Native Americans fought a losing battle against the colonists to hold on to their ancestral lands. At the close of the 19th century, the last of the Indian wars took place such as the Battle of Little Bighorn. Over time, Congress enacted laws which would entice Native Americans to settle down on a plot of land by granting them a place to live. This was called the Dawes act. Additionally, the government promised any Native American who became "civilized" that they would be entitled to citizenship as well. Thus, these enticements, along with losses on the battle front against the US army, eventually convinced them to settle down on reservations. These reservations have partial autonomy from the rest of the US and are governed by treaties until this day.

The Grange and the Populist Party

100) In the late 1800's, farmers began to band together to advocate for their rights and formed groups known as the Grange. It was successful in bringing farmers together for social and political purposes, and at its peak had over 1 million members. The Grange's power helped lower railroad prices and advocated for rural mail deliveries. Also starting in the late 1800's, a new political party called the Populist Party began to gain popularity among farmers and which advocated for free silver. This idea was to help farmers lower their debt burden by freeing up more silver and making money cheaper thus making it easier to pay back their debt. While it didn't win any Presidential elections, many of its platforms were later adapted by different parties.

REGENTS REVIEW

Use the following quotes to answer questions 1 and 2:

Speaker A: Until the 1880s, most immigrants came from the same European countries where colonial immigrants originated.

Speaker B: "New" immigrants of the late 1800s often experienced discrimination.

Speaker C: The use of a quota system is the best way to address the issues of immigration.

Speaker D: Today's immigrants take too many jobs away from those who were born in America.

1. Which two speakers are expressing an opinion related to United States immigration?
   (1) A and B
   (2) A and C
   (3) B and D
   (4) C and D

2. The "new" immigrants referred to by Speaker B came mainly from
   (1) western and northern Europe
   (2) southern and eastern Europe
   (3) Africa and Asia
   (4) Central America and South America

3. In the 1870s, the Granger movement was organized to promote the interests of
   (1) suffragists
   (2) farmers
   (3) factory workers
   (4) recent immigrants

   Kansas Fool
   We have the land to raise the wheat
   And everything that's good to eat
   And when we had no bonds or debts
   We were a jolly, happy set....
   With abundant crops raised everywhere,
   'Tis a mystery, I do declare.
   Why farmers all should fume and fret
   And why we are so deep in debt....
   — Traditional

4. What is the basic cause of the farm problem described by these song lyrics?
   (1) limits on agricultural imports
   (2) government ownership of the railroads
   (3) overproduction of farm crops
   (4) prolonged droughts in the Midwest

5. During the 1890s, many American farmers tried to resolve their economic problems by
    (1) joining the Populist Party
    (2) staging violent protests against the government
    (3) supporting government aid to railroads
    (4) asking Congress to end agricultural subsidies

6. One way in which the Chinese Exclusion Act (1882) and the Gentlemen's Agreement (1907) are similar is that they
    (1) reflected nativist attitudes in the United States
    (2) encouraged a policy of popular sovereignty
    (3) led to an increase in Asian immigration
    (4) eased requirements for citizenship

7. Which statement best expresses a common belief among nativists in the late 1800s and early 1900s?
    (1) "Give me your tired, your poor, your huddled masses."
    (2) "The streets are paved with gold."
    (3) "All immigrants strengthen America."
    (4) "America is for Americans."

8. In the late 1800s, rapid industrial development resulted in
    (1) a decrease in tariff rates
    (2) a decrease in population growth
    (3) an increase in the rate of urbanization
    (4) an increase in the price of farm products

9. Which development most clearly illustrates the nativist attitudes that existed in the United States in the 1920s?
    (1) limits on immigration established by the Quota Acts
    (2) pro-business policies of the federal government
    (3) artistic and literary achievements of the Harlem Renaissance
    (4) conflicts between religion and science as shown in the Scopes Trial

CHAPTER 16
The Progressive Movement: 1880's-1920's

The Progressive Era

101) The Progressive Era: During the late 1800's, reformers began to do battle with the many vices which had developed over the years. Great poverty, abuse, and negligence went overlooked by society as a whole but now got renewed attention. Reformers stepped out into the public sphere to demand action be taken to cure these societal ills. This was known as the Progressive Era.

102) Muckrakers: At the forefront of the movement were journalists which exposed the seamy underbelly of American life. These crusading journalists known as Muckrakers were known to the masses by their public expose`s in newspapers and books. Journalists such as Sinclair Lewis, Lincoln Steffens, Ida Tarbell and others documented stories of bad business practices that caused much misery and suffering to people. The Jungle, Lewis's most famous work, exposed the dangers of working in the Chicago meat packing industries. This exposure led to the passage of the Meat inspection Act (1906) and creation of the Food and Drug Administration (FDA-1906) that provides oversight of the private industries which do business with these items. Nellie Bly attacked the deplorable conditions of the mentally ill in Bellevue hospital. In many instances, these and other acts of public exposure helped change the public opinion and policy in America.

103) Other progressives sought to improve the housing plight of new immigrants. Philanthropists such as Jacob Riis and others involved themselves in the Social Settlement Housing. This venture was to help new immigrants by giving them housing with day care, education, and other amenities in order to help immigrants naturalize into the new country.

104) Other progressives focused their energy on peace movements. Pacifists as they were known were active in lobbying, publishing, and other forms of persuasion to bring about the end of war. These groups were particularly active before the First World War.

105) Many progressives saw the rampant drinking of the time as the cause of many societal ills and began a movement to curb drinking. This movement was called the Temperance Movement and eventually led to a constitutional amendment banning the sale of alcohol called Prohibition. However as was previously explained, being that the government was unable to stop the production and sale of alcohol, the country eventually rescinded the amendment.

106) Other progressives turned their attention towards women's rights. Some argued for the right for women to vote (universal suffrage) which they eventually won in 1920. Others argued for women's right to own property and others for the right to birth control. Eventually women won all these rights.

107) Also during this time, Jews, African Americans, and other minorities created organizations to fight for their rights. Groups such as the NAACP and the ADL were formed as defense organizations committed to fighting for African-American and Jewish rights respectively.

108) On the top of the progressive's list was the reform of government. Party bosses dominated local, state and even federal politics and their power needed to be curtailed. Up to that time, Senators were elected by the state legislatures. This lead in many instances to corruption as wealthy people bought their way into power by befriending state officials. This led some to term the Senate as the "millionaires club". Progressives pushed the 17th amendment through Congress which required that Senators be elected by popular election rather than through the states legislatures. They also demanded that corrupt politicians be removed from their posts through the institution of a recall. Furthermore, they also won the right for regular citizens to bypass politicians by voting for bills themselves called referendums and initiatives where a certain number of signatures can force an issue to be put on the ballot. Finally, they helped clean up balloting procedure by introducing the secret ballot which prevented party bosses from knowing who voted for whom.

109) After a number of years, politicians were swept up into the progressive mode and a series of progressive presidents (or presidents who made it their platform to change) arose on the political scene. It began with Theodore "Teddy" Roosevelt who ran on the platform promising every man a Square Deal or fairness. The first thing he did was to go after the large trusts which had stifled competition and created other ills. As he earned his reputation as a trustbuster, he also sought to ease tensions between business and labor by helping striking coal miners negotiate a fairer wage. He also was famous for his conservation efforts with the establishment of the US Forest Service preserving large tracts of land against development for future generations.

110) After Roosevelt's term ended, President Taft was elected president. Taft continued Roosevelt's progressive platform going after trusts and other big business practices. Yet despite some of their similarities, Taft did not have the personal magnetism that attracted many people to Roosevelt. He also took on some powerful interests and made many enemies. Being that he did not have enough political capital to defend himself against their attacks, he lost the next election to President Wilson and even drew the ire of his former mentor, President Roosevelt, who felt embarrassed by Taft's bad judgment.

111) Following Taft, President Wilson continued with Progressive policies in a policy called New Freedom. He focused his energies on establishing a Federal Trade Commission which stopped unfair trade practices before they developed into trusts. He also pushed through the Clayton Antitrust Acts which further limited trusts and unfair business practices such as "price discrimination, agreements prohibiting retailers from handling other companies' products, and directorates and agreements to control other companies"[iv]. Finally he established the Federal Reserve System in 1913, a system of banks that regulates the flow of money. Other progressives pushed for a graduated income tax in which rich people pay more taxes than poor people and which passed in 1913.

REGENTS REVIEW

1. President Theodore Roosevelt's conservation efforts were influenced by a desire to
    (1) protect natural resources for the future
    (2) increase revenues through land sales
    (3) reduce the role of the federal government
    (4) return tribal lands to Native American Indians (Aug. `12, 22, 24)

2. The actions of muckrakers in the late 19th century and early 20th century resulted in
    (1) Supreme Court decisions that expanded the right to vote
    (2) government regulation of unfair business practices
    (3) increases in the power of monopolies
    (4) reduction of the President's power to manage the economy

3. Lincoln Steffens's The Shame of the Cities and Ida Tarbell's The History of the Standard Oil Company are examples of the use of
    (1) the Gospel of Wealth
    (2) the melting pot theory
    (3) Social Darwinism
    (4) muckraking (June `12, 20, 21)

4. The Meat Inspection Act (1906) and the Pure Food and Drug Act (1906) were efforts by the federal government to
    (1) protect public health and safety
    (2) support business monopolies
    (3) restrict foreign competition
    (4) regulate child labor

    "United States Senate Criticized as 'Millionaire's Club'"

5. Which action addressed the problem suggested by this Progressive Era headline?
    (1) instituting the direct election of senators
    (2) increasing the number of senators from each state
    (3) decreasing the length of term of office for a senator
    (4) establishing voting rights for eighteen-year old Citizens

6. Ernest Hemingway, F. Scott Fitzgerald, and Sinclair Lewis were popular authors who often wrote about
    (1) the problems of urban life in the 1890s
    (2) disillusionment with American society in the 1920s
    (3) the migration of farmers in the 1930s
    (4) water and air pollution in the 1960s

"...In other words, our demand is that big business give the people a square deal and that the people give a square deal to any man engaged in big business who honestly endeavors to do what is right and proper...." (Jan`12, 22, 23)
— Theodore Roosevelt, "A Charter for Democracy,"
February 21, 1912

7. This statement reflects President Theodore Roosevelt's position that the federal government should
    (1) leave regulation of big business to the states
    (2) cease regulation of business activities
    (3) regulate abusive business practices
    (4) seize control of all trusts

8. *The Jungle,* The Octopus, and The Shame of the Cities are all books that were written to
    (1) support the formation of a new political party
    (2) promote environmental conservation
    (3) encourage reform in business and government
    (4) express opinions concerning imperialism

9. The Federal Reserve System was created in 1913 to
    (1) regulate the money supply
    (2) operate mints to coin money
    (3) collect tax revenues
    (4) protect deposits in savings banks

10. Which argument was used by Progressive Era reformers to support the use of a graduated income tax?
    (1) Imports should be taxed to make foreign goods more expensive than domestic goods.
    (2) Taxes on corporations should be reduced so jobs can be created.
    (3) People who earn more money should pay taxes at higher rates.
    (4) All citizens should be taxed at the same rate to treat all people equally.

11. The formation of the National Association for the Advancement of Colored People (NAACP) and the Anti-Defamation League (ADL) was primarily a response to
    (1) racism and prejudice
    (2) nationalism and patriotism
    (3) abolition and temperance
    (4) militarism and colonialism

12. Many of the business trusts created in the late 1800s were eventually declared illegal primarily because they
    (1) eliminated competition by forming monopolies
    (2) combined companies that manufactured different products
    (3) donated large sums of money to political candidates
    (4) allowed children to work under unsafe Conditions

13. Upton Sinclair, Frank Norris, and Ida Tarbell made their greatest contributions to the Progressive movement by
    (1) working to end political corruption in cities
    (2) speaking out for the equal rights of Hispanic Americans
    (3) supporting legislation to improve tenement housing
    (4) publishing books and articles to expose the problems of society

14. Which movement's primary goal was the ratification of a Constitutional amendment authorizing Prohibition?
    (1) abolitionist
    (2) Populist
    (3) temperance
    (4) settlement house

CHAPTER 17
The Imperialistic Age: 1880's-1920's

112) During the late 1800's-early 1900's, developing nations around the world looked for new sources of natural resources. Untapped lands around the world were conquered and placed under the rule of these developing nations (i.e. Imperialism). Although America was blessed with abundant natural resources, and their need for foreign resources was not as great as other developing countries, they, nonetheless, joined with the rest of the developing world and brought new lands under their control.

113) There were other reasons for American imperialism as well.

a. The US sought new naval bases around the world for both strategic purposes and so that they could restock their ships.

b. The US saw itself as a policeman and wished to solve humanitarian needs around the world.

c. Spreading civilization: People in the US saw an opportunity through imperialism to spread Western civilization in places which lacked it. Dubbed by supporters as the White Man's burden, it introduced roads and other benefits of western civilization to places which did not have it before.

d. Some justified imperial actions using the theory of Social Darwinism which argued that people of "higher civilization" could reasonably rule others who were not as "advanced".

114) The US imposed its rule on a number of islands and areas around the world. The US acquired Hawaii after some American sugar farmers, who wished to have their crops brought to America without paying large import tariffs, asked the US to annex Hawaii which it did in 1899. Later on, parts of Samoa were annexed and the US added the Philippines and Puerto Rico and a few other islands to its governance. While most of these places did not become a permanent part of the US, some have remained as part of the US Commonwealth (such as Puerto Rico) or other unincorporated territories (Guam, and Samoa). Others, over time, have been returned to the native peoples. Hawaii is the only territory to become a state in 1954.

115) As the US looked further east for territory, it set its sights on China and hoped to open up its borders to trade with the Open-Door Policy. This policy was to grant equal access to all foreign powers to develop spheres of influence over the Chinese. The Chinese, however, were upset over foreign intrusion in their land and

eventually a popular uprising known as the Boxer Rebellion broke out. Originally it was led by members of a nationalistic society which fought to remove the foreign influence but eventually dragged the government into the conflict as well. The Chinese lost the conflict, but despite the loss, it marked signs of Chinese resistance to foreign dominance in their country.

116) In a further demonstration of America's imperialistic ambitions, the US entered into a war with Spain over their territory of Cuba which came to be known as the Spanish American War. The war started out as a revolt of native Cubans against their Spanish overlords. The Cubans, even those not associated with the revolt, were relocated and placed into internment camps in order to root out and suppress the revolt by starving the supplies of the rebels. Some newspaper owners such as Randolph Hearst and Joseph Pulitzer seized on the opportunity to sell their newspapers by printing sensationalist accounts of the happenings, a practice known as Yellow Journalism. These accounts, coupled with a cultural attitude among many US protestants that the Spanish colonial Catholics were an immoral group who built their empire on the backs of others, helped to stir up the passions of the American public against the Spanish. When the Spanish saw the way the American newspapers covered the story, the Spanish were highly offended and a riot erupted in Havana. The US sent a battleship, The Maine, to the harbor of Havana to protect US citizens there. Under some mysterious circumstances, the ship blew up killing all 265 aboard. The US already indignant over the Spanish treatment of their colonists, and the desire of some business interests to see Cuba stable once again, caused the US to intervene militarily. The US won the war and drove the Spanish from Cuba and the Philippines. Thus, the war, besides adding to US territory for a while, established the US as a major power to be reckoned with.

117) The drive of imperialism proved to be very divisive in the US. Many argued against it stating that it was immoral and contrary to US traditions of isolationism established by President Washington. While the US continued its imperialistic drives for a number of years, by the end of WWI it was done with it.

118) During this period, the US added the Roosevelt Corollary to the Monroe Doctrine. This corollary, put in by President Teddy Roosevelt, stated that the US sees itself as a "policeman" which is to punish countries in its hemisphere who exhibit "bad" behavior. His favorite maxim was "speak softly and carry a big stick". This approach was used in other parts of the world by his administration to encourage others to follow American demands. President Taft built upon that approach with his Dollar Diplomacy. This approach sought to gain influence in Latin American countries in return for the US guaranteeing their loans. Roosevelt's Corollary was later altered by Calvin Coolidge in which he stated that only upon seeing a threat by European powers will the US intervene in the Western Hemisphere. This approach was altered again under the presidency of FDR which called for the Good Neighbor Policy in which the policy shifted from intervention to non-intervention and to reciprocal good will gestures.

REGENTS REVIEW

1. The explosion of the USS Maine and the practice of yellow journalism played a significant role in the
    (1) public's support for the Spanish-American War
    (2) creation of the Open Door policy
    (3) acquisition of Florida
    (4) purchase of Alaska (Aug. `12, 21,

2. President Theodore Roosevelt's Corollary to the Monroe Doctrine primarily affected Latin America by
    (1) guaranteeing human rights throughout the Western Hemisphere
    (2) supporting independence movements in many countries
    (3) encouraging immigration to the United States
    (4) increasing United States intervention in the Region (June `12, 22

3. Which headline related to the Spanish-American War is an example of yellow journalism?
    (1) "President McKinley Asks Congress for War Declaration Against Spain"
    (2) "United States Mobilizes for War with Spain"
    (3) "United States Demands Response to Spanish Actions"
    (4) "Spanish Troops Slaughter Innocent Cuban Citizens"

4. In the 1890s, the main goal of those who supported United States imperialism was to
    (1) bring self-government to areas under United States control
    (2) obtain overseas markets and naval bases
    (3) defend against attacks by enemy nations
    (4) spread democracy to Africa and Latin America

5. The practice of yellow journalism most directly influenced the
    (1) purchase of Alaska
    (2) acquisition of the Mexican Cession
    (3) start of the Spanish-American War
    (4) end of the Russo-Japanese War

CHAPTER 18
WWI and the Interwar Years: 1917-1941

119) In 1914, European powers divided along nationalistic lines, entered into a prolonged war which would devastate Europe. The US stayed out of the war until 1917 but entered the war in 1917 after sitting on the sidelines for 3 years. Why did they enter the war?

120) 4 reasons for the US entering the war:

a. The US had businesses interests with the English.

b. The US was attacked by German U boats, especially the famed merchant ship, the Lusitania, which was bombed by German submarines killing all those onboard after being suspect of carrying weapons for the British

c. The US had strong cultural ties with the British. The British used this affinity to their advantage by pressing forward with a propaganda campaign in the US hoping to influence the US to side with them during the war.

d. The German ambassador to Mexico, a Mr. Zimmerman, allegedly sent a note to Mexico saying that if Mexico joined them in their war effort, then the Germans would reciprocate and help them regain their territory that they lost to the Americans in the Mexican-American War.

121) This war was new in scope and scale. The US, in order to get the necessary manpower to fight the war, instituted the draft which brought millions of Americans into the army. In order take away any threat of spying by the many German expats living here, the US instituted the Wartime Espionage Acts which made it a crime to convey information about the US to an enemy, even if it was false. It also gave some police powers to the postal service. This law was challenged on the grounds that it limited free speech and led to the famous court case, Schenck v. US in which the Supreme Court ruled that in times of war (i.e. "clear and present danger") the powers of free speech can be curtailed. (Hence the famous quote from that ruling "one cannot scream fire in a crowded theater"). Also, in order to get more production out of the economy, President Wilson set up the war board industries and promoted labor-management cooperation to prevent strikes.

122) A short time after the US entered the war, the war ended. The US emerged as the only real winner and was now to be seen as a world superpower. President Wilson (the only President to hold a Ph.D.) arrived in Europe to negotiate a new world order which he hoped would lead to a more stable world. The plan that he came

with was called the 14 Points plan which he had previously delivered to Congress. In it, amongst other points, he called for the end of the arms race, an end to colonial fighting, the establishment of a League of Nations, no secret treaties, and open trade and sea ways. While some points were never adopted, the idea of the League of Nations did eventually become a reality when the UN was established after World War II.

123) As peace dawned over Europe, the allies signed the Treaty of Versailles. This treaty called for the complete demilitarization of Germany, and fines to repay debt accumulated during the war. Back home, the US senate refused to ratify the Treaty of Versailles because of isolationist reasons (i.e. the fear of being pulled into another war in Europe) and so instead signed a separate pact with Germany. The feeling of isolationism was strengthened by the Neutrality Acts of the 1930's which sought to cut off the US from world involvement.

124) Economy and culture following the war: Following the war the US economy picked up at a tremendous pace. This pickup was largely due to the stimulation brought about by the war and continued through the 1920's. These years, known as years of Coolidge Prosperity or the Roaring Twenties, saw the rise of new modes of dress and culture. Young women began to dress in provocative fashions (for those times) and were labeled Flappers. Jazz music arrived which was heavily influenced by African rhythms. African American culture flourished in NYC in what was called the Harlem Renaissance. People such as Duke Ellington (jazz musician), Langston Hughes (poetry) Bessie Smith (blues singer) made their mark on America's cultural scene. This renaissance came about after the Great Migration in which thousands of African Americans from the South flooded into cities in the North having been denied their rights and economic opportunities in the Jim Crow south. The migration brought about a marked cultural change to the predominantly white city. Also, during this period, following the Russian Communist revolution, some people in the US were influenced by the ideas of the revolution and produced the first Red Scare (fear of communism spreading here) in the 1920's. There were some famous high-profile raids such as the Palmer Raids in 1919 where hundreds of suspected communists and anarchists were rounded up and deported. Finally during this time a cultural debate sprung up in the US over the teaching of Evolution in public schools. Religious people argued that it isn't science and should be banned from schools. The resulting fighting brought the issue to court in the Scopes trial where it was deemed to be a science and allowed to be taught.

The Great Depression

125) The Great Depression: While the Roaring twenties, as they were called, saw a spike of wealth, it didn't necessarily translate into improved economic conditions for everyone. Many workers still earned low wages, worked long hours, and in dangerous conditions. Disasters such as the triangle shirtwaist factory, which killed many, raised awareness about the miserable working conditions faced by millions of Americans. Furthermore, the economy exhibited weakness in major areas.

A. The economy was still on a war time setting despite the end of the "Great War" and was thus produced more than it was selling. This is called overproduction. Stagnation and inventory rose because of the overproduction, unsettling many companies.

B. The practice at the time was to sell stocks based on margin which meant that people could buy stock but not have to pay cash for it up front. This meant that they would owe the money to the seller and hope the stock would go up and then have money to repay it. When the true value of companies became known, the stock market crashed in October of 1929 erasing any creditor's hopes of ever recovering their money. Seeing all this instability in the economy, people were gripped by a panic that their money was not secure and ran to the banks to recover it. This caused a run on the banks with hordes of people lining up at the banks to pull out their money which caused banks to run out of money. Additionally, when the true value of the companies hit home, millions were laid off and money that was invested in these companies was lost. To make matters even worse, during the 1930's great dust storms and droughts hit the Midwest and West causing millions of dollars in losses for farmers in what became known as the Dust Bowl.

126) In the meantime, the government stayed on the sidelines not wishing to interfere in the economy. President Coolidge was pro-business and promised, that with time, things would improve. However, instead of conditions improving over time, they worsened with millions going hungry and homeless. Millions roamed the streets and countryside looking for work and food, with unemployment reaching a staggering 30%. The next president, President Hoover, did little to try and change the situation. Homeless people formed tent cities and renamed them Hoovervilles after President Hoover did little to improve the lives of millions. It wasn't until F.D.R was elected President and implemented the New Deal, along with millions being spent on fighting WWII, did things finally start looking up economically.

REGENTS REVIEW

1. **The United States Senate refused to ratify the Treaty of Versailles after World War I because many senators believed**
    (1) President Woodrow Wilson was too ill to sign the treaty
    (2) most Americans had sympathized with Germany during the war
    (3) the treaty would not require reparations from Germany
    (4) the League of Nations could draw the United States into future wars (Aug. `12 , 25, 26)

2. **What was one feature of the United States economy during the 1920s that contributed to the Great Depression?**
    (1) increase in federal regulation
    (2) expansion of easy credit
    (3) growth of the trade deficit
    (4) influence of foreign corporations

3. **Duke Ellington, Langston Hughes, and Bessie Smith are most closely associated with efforts to**
    (1) expand the Back to Africa movement
    (2) fight discrimination through the judicial system
    (3) promote the cultural identity of African Americans through the arts
    (4) establish the National Association for the Advancement of Colored People

4. **The Red Scare, the growth of the Ku Klux Klan, and the murder convictions of Sacco and Vanzetti were influenced by**
    (1) the rise of organized crime
    (2) the passage of immigration quota acts
    (3) a distrust of foreigners
    (4) an effort to stop fascism (June `12, 25, 28, 49

5. **What was a basic cause of the Great Depression of the 1930s?**
    (1) Too many antitrust laws were passed.
    (2) Tariffs on foreign manufactured goods were reduced.
    (3) The distribution of income was unequal.
    (4) Immigration was not limited.

6. **The Supreme Court decision in Schenck v. United States (1919) and the passage of the USA Patriot Act (2001) demonstrate the principle that the federal government can**
    (1) guarantee citizens the right to bear arms
    (2) restrict the power of the President
    (3) limit individual rights in times of national emergency
    (4) expand the liberties protected by the Bill of Rights

7. During World War I, President Woodrow Wilson used his wartime powers to
    (1) win passage of quota acts (Jan `12, 25, 26
    (2) grant all women the right to vote
    (3) expand freedom of the press
    (4) increase government control of the economy

8. The Senate's opposition to United States membership in the League of Nations was based mainly on the
    (1) cost of membership dues
    (2) failure to give the United States veto power
    (3) fear of being drawn into future wars
    (4) concern that United States businesses would be damaged

9. The division in public opinion over the Scopes trial and Prohibition demonstrates which characteristic of the 1920s?
    (1) discrimination against immigrants
    (2) clash of cultural values
    (3) fear of international communism
    (4) opposition to the Ku Klux Klan

10. During the 1930s, poor land management and severe drought conditions across parts of the Midwest resulted in the
    (1) formation of the United States Department of Agriculture
    (2) creation of wheat surpluses
    (3) growth of the Granger movement
    (4) development of Dust Bowl conditions on the Great Plains

> (11-12) We intend to begin on the first of February unrestricted submarine warfare. We shall endeavor in spite of this to keep the United States of America neutral. In the event of this not succeeding, we make Mexico a proposal of alliance on the following basis: make war together, make peace together, generous financial support and an understanding on our part that Mexico is to reconquer the lost territory in Texas,
> New Mexico, and Arizona. The settlement in detail is left to you....
> — Telegram of January 19, 1917

11. This telegram was part of an effort to
    (1) form an alliance between Germany and the United States
    (2) convince several western states to secede from the United States
    (3) bring Mexico into World War I on the side of Great Britain and France
    (4) enlist Mexican support for Germany if the United States declared war

12. **Publication of this telegram in United States newspapers helped to**
    (1) reelect Woodrow Wilson as President
    (2) convince the American public to support entrance into World War I
    (3) encourage Congress to pass neutrality legislation
    (4) grant statehood to Arizona and New Mexico

13. **Henry Cabot Lodge and other senators opposed ratification of the Treaty of Versailles (1919) because they believed the treaty**
    (1) failed to punish Germany for its involvement in World War I
    (2) excluded reparations for European allies
    (3) could draw the United States into future conflicts
    (4) placed blame for World War I on all the warring countries

14. **What was the primary reason many African Americans migrated to the North both during and after World War I?**
    (1) More economic opportunities existed in the North.
    (2) Few chances to gain political office were available in the South.
    (3) Racism and discrimination had been eliminated in the North.
    (4) Southern cities were overcrowded.

15. **The Harlem Renaissance of the 1920s most enhanced American culture by**
    (1) pressuring southern states to extend voting rights
    (2) expanding African American access to education
    (3) popularizing African American contributions to the arts
    (4) convincing the Supreme Court to allow affirmative action

16. **Which action was a result of the other three?**
    (1) Germany's policy of unrestricted submarine warfare
    (2) United States entry into World War I
    (3) interception of the Zimmermann Note
    (4) United States loans to Allied nations

17. **The vote by the United States Senate on the Treaty of Versailles (1919) demonstrated**
    (1) an unwillingness to join the League of Nations
    (2) a commitment to collective security
    (3) a belief that the nation required a stronger military
    (4) a rejection of colonialism

CHAPTER 19
The New Deal and WWII: 1930's-1945

127) As the crisis grew within the American economy, pressure began to build on politicians to do something. Some focused on immigrants and argued that constraints should be placed on immigration in the hope that it would keep the jobs within the native population. Additionally, people reasoned that by holding back immigration, it would reduce the rate of impoverished peoples entering, and reduce the burden to be shouldered by the majority. Yet what people wanted most was that the government intervene somehow to help the citizens. With the election of FDR, this governmental action began to take shape.

New Deal

128) New Deal: FDR proposed a series of measures called the New Deal which were designed to stimulate the economy with government sponsored jobs, increased regulation and a safety net for the most vulnerable. These ideas translated into many programs, such as, but not limited to:

- **creating jobs** through the creation of a worker's program (the WPA),
- **the Tennessee Valley Administration** that was set up to plan regional development,
- **NRA**, a voluntary organization that provided guidelines to businesses on what is fair business practices, and awarded those that complied with a tag/seal to proclaim that their company was NRA compliant,
- **FDIC insurance:** a government guarantee that all money deposited in a bank would be insured by the government in case of a collapse of that bank up to 10 thousand dollars per account (now increased to 100 thousand dollars per account) and which helped shore up the banking industries,
- **created the AAA** which put heavy taxes on farmers who produced staple crops or gave them payments not to plant certain crops. These incentives and taxes helped decrease the number of crops produced which then raised the revenue for farmers and pushed them to diversify their crops.
- **CCC or the Civilian Conservation Corps** which trained unemployed workers to work in conservation (parks etc.)
- **Social security** - to provide a safety net for the elderly with economic support for the most vulnerable of Americans.

129) **Court packing:** Over time, lawsuits challenging the constitutionality of programs such as the AAA were brought to court. Business leaders were particularly upset at many of the programs for they infringed on their territory. In many cases, the courts ruled that the administration's programs were un-constitutional. As tensions increased between the Court and the administration, FDR threatened to pack the Supreme Court (called court packing) with pro big-business jurists (as it does not say in the constitution how many Supreme Court judges there must be) who would not oppose the goals of the administration. The court eventually backed off and the threat was never carried out. Over time the economy began to stabilize but did not fully recover or reach full employment until the US entered WWII.

130) When WWII broke out in 1938, the US officially remained neutral and the sentiment in the country largely isolationist. In 1940 the US began assisting the Allies in Europe in line with FDR's policy that the US needs to be the "great arsenal of democracy". However, the US did not formally enter the conflict itself until the bombing of Pearl Harbor by the Japanese in December of 1941 which brought the US into conflict with the Axis powers. The US fought a few major operations at once. At first, they brought the fight into Italy and conquered it with the other Allies. Once that they had the south of Europe conquered, the Russians pushed in from the east and the US and its allies plotted a push from the west. The famous landing at Normandy, France on D-Day marked the beginning of the end of Hitler's regime. After months of heavy fighting, which included massive aerial bombardments and dogfights, the allies finally cornered the Germans and bombed Berlin until it was utterly destroyed. The Germans finally gave up. However, the Japanese were still putting up a tenacious fight in the Pacific despite the punishing air bombardments on Japanese cities by the US Air force. Fortunately, by that time, the US, with the help of famous German-Jewish scientists, had built the atom bomb in a secretive program called the Manhattan Project. With US patience running thin and fear of massive loss of life by US soldiers if they would have to invade Japan, the decision was made by President Truman (Pres. Roosevelt died during the war and his Vice President, Harry Truman took over) to drop the atomic bomb on the Japanese obliterating two major Japanese cities and finally forcing their surrender. Thus, the war was over.

131) Prior to the close of the war, the heads of the Allies met in Yalta (called the Yalta Conference) to discuss the reorganization of post-war Europe. They agreed at the conference, to establish the UN of which all countries would take part. They also agreed to divide Germany into 4 parts and established boundaries for countries among other things. After the war, these leaders met again at Potsdam, Germany in what became known as the Potsdam Conference to determine the process of how to demilitarize and de-Nazify Germany.

132) Following the war, the US and world leaders established a tribunal called the Nuremberg Trials to try the Nazi leaders and sentence them for the war crimes that they committed. They also established the UN and declared later on in 1948 that genocide was a crime against humanity that must be stopped.

133) After playing active roles during the war, women and African Americans coming home after the war, sought greater rights for themselves. During the war, women played an integral role in the military war effort as technicians working in factories to build weaponry, and as nurses tending to the wounded in the field. African Americans also contributed as soldiers fighting alongside white Americans. For their sacrifice,

they demanded that their rights be recognized. While things did not immediately improve, they were granted their demands later on in the 1960's and 70's.

134) During the war, the US was concerned that the large Japanese population on the west coast of the US would turn against the America. To combat this, they moved all Americans of Japanese descent to internment camps for the duration of the war. These camps, while not concentration camps, nonetheless violated the rights of these citizens. A Japanese American brought a lawsuit against the government called Korematsu vs. the US but lost. In the 1980's, the US formally apologized for its behavior during the war and repaid those who were interned in those camps and their descendants 20 thousand dollars apiece.

135) During the war, the US imposed food rationing and price controls in order to keep prices down, and supply limited, so that production of goods and services could go towards the war effort. Furthermore, the US encouraged people to grow their own food in their gardens called victory gardens to supplement the food available.

REGENTS REVIEW

- Banning loans to nations at war
- Prohibiting the sale of armaments to nations at war
- Limiting travel by United States citizens on ships of belligerent nations

1. These governmental actions of the 1930s were similar in that each was intended to:
    (1) support efforts of the Munich Conference
    (2) protect United States colonies from foreign aggression
    (3) limit the influence of Japan in Asia
    (4) keep the United States out of international conflicts (Aug. `12, 31, 34)

2. The major reason for President Harry Truman's decision to use atomic bombs against Japan was the
    (1) potential loss of American lives from an invasion of Japan
    (2) need to defeat Japan before defeating Germany
    (3) plan to bring democratic government to Japan after the war
    (4) failure of the island-hopping campaign against Japan

    …War criminals and those who have participated in planning or carrying out Nazi enterprises involving or resulting in atrocities or war crimes shall be arrested and brought to judgment. Nazi leaders, influential Nazi supporters and high officials of Nazi organizations and institutions and any other persons dangerous to the occupation or its objectives shall be arrested and interned.…
    — Protocol of the Proceedings, Potsdam Conference, August 1945

3. This agreement made at the Potsdam Conference led directly to the
    (1) creation of the North Atlantic Treaty Organization (NATO)
    (2) trials in Nuremberg, Germany
    (3) announcement of the Truman Doctrine
    (4) division of Germany into occupation zones

4. During the Great Depression of the 1930s and the economic crisis of 2008–2010, the federal government initiated reforms in the banking system to
    (1) strengthen federal control over the financial system
    (2) eliminate the flow of capital to foreign countries
    (3) promote laissez-faire business practices
    (4) provide for a more equitable distribution of wealth

5. President Franklin D. Roosevelt said the United States needed to become the "great arsenal of democracy" mainly because he was trying to
    (1) increase the number of Supreme Court justices
    (2) assist the Allied nations
    (3) limit the influence of the defense industry
    (4) gain public support for a third term (June `12, 30, 31)

6. The Nuremberg War Crimes trials of 1945–1949 established the international precedent that
    (1) the United States should avoid commitments with foreign nations
    (2) military leaders cannot be held responsible for wartime actions
    (3) individuals may be tried for crimes against humanity
    (4) soldiers must obey an order even if it conflicts with basic humanitarian values

7. What was the goal of President Franklin D. Roosevelt's plan to add more justices to the Supreme Court? (Jan `12, 30, 31, 33)
    (1) to help the Supreme Court implement its decisions
    (2) to limit judicial opposition to New Deal programs
    (3) to convince Congress to enact new economic laws
    (4) to replace the Chief Justice of the Supreme Court

8. To help win World War II, the federal government found it necessary to
    (1) return to the gold standard
    (2) outlaw labor unions
    (3) impose rationing and price controls
    (4) integrate the military

9. During World War II, Japanese Americans were sent to internment centers primarily because they
    (1) were considered illegal aliens
    (2) had been convicted of spying for Japan
    (3) refused to enlist in the United States military
    (4) were thought to be threats to national security

10. Consumer rationing was used during World War II as a way to
    (1) increase exploration for natural resources
    (2) limit supplies of weapons to American allies
    (3) draft men into the armed forces
    (4) ensure that the military had essential Materials

11. **During World War II, the Manhattan Project was the name of the plan to**
    (1) open a second front in Europe
    (2) capture Pacific islands held by the Japanese
    (3) develop the atomic bomb
    (4) liberate German concentration camps

12. **Women played a major role on the domestic front during World War II by**
    (1) becoming candidates for public office
    (2) campaigning for woman's suffrage
    (3) demonstrating against involvement in the war
    (4) taking jobs in the defense industry

13. **President Abraham Lincoln's suspension of habeas corpus and President Franklin D. Roosevelt's executive order forcing Japanese Americans into internment camps both demonstrate that**
    (1) Constitutional rights can be limited during times of war
    (2) Congress can pass laws limiting the power of a strong President
    (3) immigrants are protected by the same Constitutional rights as United States citizens
    (4) Presidential actions must be submitted to the Supreme Court for approval

CHAPTER 20
The Cold War: 1947-1991

136) WWII, world powers set up the UN to try and resolve conflicts through peaceful negotiations. The UN has a General Assembly which is largely a symbolic body with little policy influence while most major issues are resolved by the UN Security Council. The Security Council has 5 permanent members with veto powers: US, Russia, France, England and China and 14 members altogether.

The Cold War

137) The Cold War was a state of tension between Russia and the US that began almost immediately following the conclusion of WWII. These former allies, who both had occupied Berlin, quickly split into rivals as ideological differences between them bubbled over. The split took on a serious tone as the Russians blockaded Berlin and refused entry to the US into East Germany where Berlin was located. The US needed to get supplies to their troops stationed in West Berlin and they did so by airlift (called the Berlin Airlift). Over time this crisis dissipated as the parties agreed to a route linking east and west Berlin, and which allowed supplies to transfer from West Germany to Berlin. Many Germans living in East Berlin attempted to cross over from their side to the American side. The Russians embarrassed by the defections, built a wall (called the Berlin Wall) dividing the two Berlins which would not allow Germans to move from one side to the other. This wall symbolized the conflict as it showcased the divide between the US and Russia.

The Domino Theory

138) The Russians annexed some of the states in their path to Germany and they were made into satellite countries under Russian control. The US feared the spread of communism and argued that if one country "caught" the contagion of communism then other countries near it would also "catch it". This theory, known as the Domino Theory held sway throughout much of the cold war.

Containment and Truman Doctrine

139) The US (under the Truman doctrine) sought to contain the spread of communism and developed a two-pronged approach called containment. In it, the US used a mixture of incentives and military aid to stop the spread of communism. The US gave out billions of dollars to rebuild parts of West Germany and Western Europe that were devastated by the war in what was called the Marshall Plan. During President Eisenhower's reign, the plan also extended to the Middle East in which the US sent military aid or economic assistance to those in the Middle East seeking to stop the advancement of communism in their country. The US also formed an alliance between themselves and the rest of the Western Europe in what was called NATO. This treaty said that an attack on one of its member states would be considered an attack on all the states.

140) The US concerned about radical communists at home reacted in various ways to curb the perceived threat. The Taft Hartley Act of 1947 sought to de-radicalize the unions by eliminating radicals from union leadership and limiting the power of the unions by narrowing the types of strikes and picketing. It also allowed the government to ban strikes altogether if they imperiled the safety and health of the country.

141) In order to examine the issue of communism in America in greater detail, the House of Representatives set up a committee to investigate un-American activities. In the Senate, Senator McCarthy from Wisconsin used his power to call hearings in which he publicly interrogated supposed communists and tried to place them in a bad light. This occurred at the time when a new red scare was playing out in the US. This scare was caused by the Algiers Hiss case in which Hiss (an employee at the state department) was accused of spying for the Soviets while working their. Another incident, the Rosenberg Affair, in which Julius and Ethel Rosenberg allegedly sold nuclear secrets to the Russians and which led them to develop the hydrogen bomb, also brought about an atmosphere of fear in the US. However, McCarthy was soon discredited after it apparent that he used his committee as a personal tool to settle old political scores, among other abuses and gaffs. The HUAC, (House Un-American Activities Committee), in the House of Representatives which also investigated supposed communist subversions was also eventually shut down.

142) The first war that the US entered in the quest to stop the further spread of communism was the Korean War. This war (which technically speaking has never ended) was to prevent the spread of communism from North Korea to South Korea. The war ended in a stalemate between the North and the South. The zone where the two sides stopped fighting is known as the Demilitarized Zone (the DMZ in short) and is still heavily guarded on both sides of the border. General Macarthur, who was a storied General in WWII, was dismissed from his post as General of the Korean War after he publicly aired his disagreements over the course of the war with President Truman.

143) After the 1950's, the Russians developed their own nuclear weapons and an arms race ensued. Both sides developed massive nuclear weapons stockpiles and aimed ICBM's (ballistic missiles) at each other which were capable of M.A.D. or Mutually Assured Destruction. The US developed a strategy of brinkmanship which said that the US will push the other side to the brink of war and then back off. This policy was employed in the hope that it would show the USSR how serious we were and prevent the further spread of communism. This policy created a great deal of stress in the US during that era as people prepared and feared the worst. There were some close calls as well. The Cuban Missile Crisis, began after the US led a failed coup attempt, called the Bay of Pigs invasion, against Cuba's newly elected communist leader Fidel Castro in 1961. As tensions rose between the US and Cuba, the Cubans called on their ideological ally, the USSR, to help them. The Soviets sent the Cubans ICBM's in 1962. President Kennedy ordered the missiles out of Cuba's vicinity within three days or we would fire first. The Russians backed down at the last moment and a disaster was averted. Another incident, the U-2 incident in 1960 where an American spy plane was shot down by the Russians, caused a great deterioration in US-USSR relations.

144) In the mid 1950's, a soviet satellite named Sputnik was launched. This was a historic event since it was the first time a manmade object circled the earth. The US looked on in alarm as the threat of Russian superiority in the sciences and math frightened the US into believing the Russians were forging ahead and we were falling behind. A massive increase in math and science funding ensued and the US soon led the world in innovation and technology.

145) In the 1960's and 70's the US entered into another cold war conflict, the Vietnam War. In this war, the US was "attacked" in the Gulf of Tonkin off the coast of Vietnam purportedly by North Vietnamese who were communist. The President then ordered an attack on Vietnam after the Gulf of Tonkin Resolution was passed which authorized the President to respond to the needs of the hour in Southeast Asia without receiving prior authorization from Congress. As the war dragged on however, it became clear to Congress that they needed to get a handle on the length of the war and limited it in the war powers act which said that the President can react but must get authorization after 60 days for the war to continue.

REGENTS REVIEW

1. **Which event marked the beginning of the space race with the Soviet Union?**
   - (1) U-2 spy plane incident
   - (2) launch of Sputnik
   - (3) Berlin airlift
   - (4) creation of the space shuttle program

2. **The Berlin airlift was used during the Cold War to**
   - (1) rescue people fleeing West Germany
   - (2) prevent a communist takeover of Greece and Turkey
   - (3) overcome a blockade created by the Soviet Union
   - (4) support peacekeeping efforts by the North Atlantic Treaty Organization (NATO)

   (June `12, 33, 34)

3. **McCarthyism in the 1950s is most closely associated with**
   - (1) claims that communists had infiltrated the federal government
   - (2) efforts to prevent pro-communist governments in Latin America
   - (3) formation of the Warsaw Pact
   - (4) passage of the Interstate Highway Act

4. **The principal goal of the United Nations has been to**
   - (1) develop military alliances around the world
   - (2) encourage expansion of international trade
   - (3) promote peaceful solutions to world problems
   - (4) regulate the use of atomic energy

5. **Which of these events related to space exploration occurred first?**
   - (1) Neil Armstrong walking on the Moon
   - (2) development of the space shuttle
   - (3) John Glenn orbiting Earth
   - (4) launching of Sputnik

6. **Which statement about the Marshall Plan is most accurate?**
   - (1) It was used to finance rearmament after World War II.
   - (2) It was denied to all former World War II enemies.
   - (3) It was used to rebuild European nations after World War II.
   - (4) It was given to all African and Asian allies during the Cold War.

7) The Hungarian uprising of 1956, the U-2 incident, and the Cuban missile crisis led to
   (1) military actions by the Southeast Asia Treaty Organization (SEATO)
   (2) increased tensions between the United States and the Soviet Union
   (3) international efforts to control communist China
   (4) creation of the Warsaw Pact

> "Attorney General Palmer Deports 249 Foreigners"(1919)
> "Nixon Accuses Alger Hiss of Espionage" (1948)
> "Rosenbergs Executed for Treason" (1953)

8. Each of these headlines demonstrates that during the 20th century
   (1) the rights of the accused were expanded
   (2) membership rose dramatically in groups considered to be subversive
   (3) censorship was a primary policy of the government
   (4) fear of communist activities prompted government actions

CHAPTER 21
1945-1975: Economic, Social and Cultural Change

Post-World War II

146) Post-World War II: The economy bounced back at full speed after the devastating depression of the 1930's. This bounce, which came during the Eisenhower years, was achieved in tandem with great innovations in home appliances such as modern refrigerators and washing machines. The GI Bill granted young soldiers free college tuition and other benefits if they fought in WWII. It was also a time of great social conformity. Religion was considered a standard for every household and middle-class values were promoted. In addition, many babies were born after millions of young soldiers and sailors came back and had children in what's has become known as the baby boom.

147) Amongst the greatest changes that accompanied the post war years was the popularity of the automobile and with it the growth of the suburbs. With great gusto, Americans grabbed onto this mode of transportation and with it a major flight from cities occurred. Highways now teemed with cars between cities and suburbs as people were able to move from home to work with great ease. In addition, many veterans returning from the war looked for a place to settle and found it in the suburbs. The new houses were built and bought on consumer credit and promoted by the federal government which made the purchase of a home the American dream.

148) Yet underneath the surface of what looked like a very placid America, there were great areas of discontent with young people searching for real meaning and connection. In the south, African Americans still suffered severe discrimination in almost every arena of life and women were still discriminated against as well. Rising from these frustrations, tensions began to boil as the 1950's moved forward and civil rights became a prominent issue in American public life.

149) What galvanized a budding civil rights movement was the Supreme Court decision in 1954 called Brown vs. the Bd. of Education of Topeka, Kansas. The court, under the liberal aegis of Judge Earl Warren, ruled that the century old policy of segregation of public schools was illegal by ruling that separate but equal is unequal. This fateful decision emboldened African Americans who lived in the south to challenge the status quo of the day and demand that their children be taught together with white children. Nine parents of African American children enrolled their kids in white schools in Little Rock,

Arkansas and challenged the status quo. When white parents and activists threatened the safety of the students, and their Governor Orval Faubus unwilling to comply with the law, President Eisenhower ordered the army to stand guard and protect the students. This act showed the government's determination to stand down racism and fight for equality and the rule of law as interpreted by the Supreme Court.

150) Once this issue was fought for and won by the African American community, it began to tackle the big issue: segregation in public life. The first arena was the Montgomery Bus Boycott. This began when a young African American female activist, Rosa Parks, refused to stand up and move to the "colored" part of the bus. She was arrested and charged for violating the public order. Activists immediately called for a boycott of the Montgomery bus system and instead walked or hitched to work. This boycott worked and spread from Montgomery, Alabama to other cities and states in the South. In particular, activists took "Freedom Rides" on interstate buses in which black and white people sat together on buses in violation of public law. These activists were arrested, harassed, and attacked yet they never fought back.

151) The emphasis on a non-violent approach exhibited by these activists were encouraged by the leading voice in the African American protest movement, Martin Luther King Jr. He and other activists called on protesters to follow Mohandas Gandhi's role in breaking colonialism in India by engaging in non-violence and civil disobedience. This turned out to be a fateful call. Many African Americans followed Dr. King's call and were beaten while protesting racist laws but didn't fight back. In Greensboro, South Carolina many African American activists sat in on white lunch counters and demanded that they be served like white Americans. When the police came to arrest the violators, the activists refused to leave and were beaten. On many occasions the press covered these sit-ins and when the protesters were beaten, the actions were caught on TV and photos bringing cries of protest from many corners of American society.

152) The civil rights movement grew and grew through the early 1960's. In August of 1963 Dr. King led a major march on Washington in which hundreds of thousands of people participated and where he called on the need for change. It was at this protest that he gave his famous "I have a dream" speech which came to symbolize the dreams of the civil rights movement. Another approach which was less popular and more controversial was the Black Power Movement led by Malcolm X and others. They advocated a militant approach to change and argued that without it, nothing will change. In 1965, Malcolm X was assassinated by members of the Nation of Islam which he had left the year before.

Women's Rights

153) Women's rights substantially increased during this period. The modern Feminist Movement was born during this age in which women as a group demanded equal rights. Many women's organizations arose during this period such as NOW (National Organization of Women) and others which support women's rights. In the 1960's the invention of the birth control pill gave women more control over their reproductive lives than they ever had. In 1973 the Supreme Court ruled in Roe V. Wade that abortion was legal and that no state could ban its practice. This furthered the cause of the feminists who wished to empower women despite its controversial nature.

Civil Rights Act

154) Eventually public opinion turned against Southern segregation laws. Landmark legislation called the Civil Rights Act of 1964 was signed under President Lyndon B. Johnson, who took over for President Kennedy after he was shot and killed in 1963. These laws outlawed any public discrimination based on race, color, ethnicity, religion or gender. With this legislation and others later on, groups that were historically discriminated against also achieved equality through legislation. Jews, Native Americans, and the physically handicapped fought for equal protection and rights and which they eventually won.

155) Another major issue during this period was the Vietnam War. As in the Korean War, this war, which began to prevent the North Vietnamese from conquering South Vietnam, eventually turned into a nightmare for American troops. When a draft was instituted to induct more troops into service, many Americans began to see the war as immoral and protested US involvement. This war which coincided with the birth of the Hippie Movement (which rejected the values of 1950's America), began to tear the country apart. Many people began sit-ins on college campuses to protest US involvement in the war. Draft dodgers burnt their draft cards and fled the country while crippling protests gripped an already divided nation. Eventually, Pres. Nixon under intense domestic pressure, pulled out of Vietnam in 1973 after thousands of troops were killed. Soon after the US pulled out of South Vietnam, the south fell to Communist forces.

156) The 1960's also brought about great cultural changes and debates. Conservative traditional values fell to the wayside as young adults questioned the culture and morality of society around them. Young people began dressing differently and growing their hair long. A new genre of music inspired by African beats emerged called "rock n' roll" and came to define the new mood that these young people were experiencing. They adopted a more liberal attitude towards mores and values than the older more conservative generation had. They challenged conventional thinking about race, religion, gender roles, war and peace, morality and authority in general. The clash between parents and children became known as the generation gap. Acting on the mood of "peace" in the air, young people joined movements such as the Peace Corp, a government sponsored program which supports building communities all over the globe. To add to the mix of experiment and newness, a new drug developed by a chemist called LSD became very popular among this young exploratory crowd. However, over time, the substance was banned as it, along with other addictive substances, highlighted the growing problems with drug addiction in America.

157) This generation and its liberal tendencies eventually inspired politicians as well. In the 1960's, President Johnson pushed through congress a liberal agenda called the Great Society, a part of which was his declared War on Poverty. It attempted to erase poverty in the US by creating entitlement programs such as Medicare for the elderly, Medicaid for the poor, welfare (money) grants for the poor, Food Stamps for the poor, HUD (subsidized housing) for the poor and other programs designed to ease the effects of poverty on poor people in America. Another initiative called Affirmative Action was aimed at raising the socioeconomic level of African Americans by giving them preferences in admissions to schools and colleges etc. However, this idea has proven very controversial as white people have complained of reverse discrimination.

REGENTS REVIEW

1. Which factor directly contributed to the growth of suburban communities after World War II?
   (1) Mass transit systems closed.
   (2) Property taxes were eliminated in many towns.
   (3) Returning veterans created a demand for housing.
   (4) Widespread mortgage foreclosures caused farmers to leave rural areas. (Aug. `12, 37, 38, 39, 40)

   > May 13, 1958
   > The President
   > The White House
   > Washington, D. C.
   >
   > My dear Mr. President:
   > I was sitting in the audience at the Summit Meeting of Negro [African-American] Leaders yesterday when you said we must have patience. On hearing you say this, I felt like standing up and saying, "Oh no! Not again." …17 million Negroes cannot do as you suggest and wait for the hearts of men to change. We want to enjoy now the rights that we feel we are entitled to as Americans. This we cannot do unless we pursue aggressively goals which all other Americans achieved over 150 years ago. As the chief executive of our nation, I respectfully suggest that you unwittingly crush the spirit of freedom in Negroes by constantly urging forbearance [delay] and give hope to those pro-segregation leaders like Governor [Orval] Faubus who would take from us even those freedoms we now enjoy. Your own experience with Governor Faubus is proof enough that forbearance and not eventual integration is the goal the pro-segregation leaders seek.…
   > Respectfully yours,
   > Jackie Robinson
   > Source: National Archives & Records Administration

2. Which action by the federal government would Jackie Robinson most likely have supported to achieve his stated goals?
   (1) federal assistance to expand segregated facilities
   (2) creation of additional job training programs
   (3) appointment of a commission to study the causes of urban race riots
   (4) faster implementation of the decision in Brown v. Board of Education of Topeka (1954)

3. When Jackie Robinson mentions President Dwight D. Eisenhower's experience with Governor Faubus, he is referring to the action the President took in
    (1) hiring minority workers to build the interstate highway system
    (2) sending federal troops to Central High School in Little Rock, Arkansas
    (3) supporting the Montgomery bus boycott
    (4) ordering that all military bases located in southern states be integrated

4. A major goal of the Great Society programs begun under President Lyndon B. Johnson was to
    (1) stimulate oil production in the United States
    (2) provide tax concessions to manufacturers
    (3) reduce poverty in the nation
    (4) increase the size of the armed forces

5. The GI Bill helped soldiers who served in World War II by
    (1) mandating integration of the military
    (2) funding college education for veterans
    (3) requiring women to surrender their wartime jobs to men
    (4) eliminating union seniority rules that hurt Veterans

> …It is important that the reasons for my action be understood by all our citizens. As you know, the Supreme Court of the United States has decided that separate public educational facilities for the races are inherently unequal and therefore compulsory school segregation laws are unConstitutional….
> — President Dwight D. Eisenhower, September 24, 1957

6. Which Supreme Court case is referred to in this quotation?
    (1) Dred Scott v. Sanford
    (2) Brown v. Board of Education of Topeka
    (3) Heart of Atlanta Motel v. United States
    (4) Tinker v. Des Moines School District(june`12, 35, 36, 37, 38

7. Which action did President Dwight D. Eisenhower take to enforce this Supreme Court decision?
    (1) ordering the closing of Central High School in Little Rock, Arkansas
    (2) sending United States Army troops to enforce school integration
    (3) proposing legislation in support of school segregation
    (4) transferring white students to a new public high school

8. Which action is the best example of the use of civil disobedience?
    (1) passing the Voting Rights Act of 1965
    (2) lobbying Congress to eliminate the poll tax
    (3) attending a political rally in Iowa
    (4) conducting sit-ins at restaurants in the South

Base your answer to question 9 on the song lyrics below and on your knowledge of social studies.

> … Come mothers and fathers
> Throughout the land
> And don't criticize
> What you can't understand
> Your sons and your daughters
> Are beyond your command
> Your old road is
> Rapidly agin'.
> Please get out of the new one
> If you can't lend your hand
> For the times they are a-changin'…
> — Bob Dylan, "The Times They Are A-Changin'," 1963

9. Which concern of the 1960s is being commented on by the author of these lyrics?
    (1) rural poverty   (2) adult illiteracy
    (3) environmental protection (4) the generation gap

10. Since the end of World War II (1945), what has been a major effect of population change in the United States?
    (1) The Social Security system went bankrupt.
    (2) Demand for medical facilities has declined.
    (3) A surplus of unskilled workers has led to decreased immigration.
    (4) Suburban areas have grown faster than cities

> "… And so, my fellow Americans: ask not what your country can do for you—ask what you can do for your country.…"
> — President John F. Kennedy, Inaugural Address, January 20, 1961

11. Which action by President John F. Kennedy was most consistent with the challenge included in this statement?
    (1) forming the Peace Corps
    (2) negotiating the Nuclear Test Ban Treaty
    (3) supporting the Bay of Pigs invasion
    (4) visiting the Berlin Wall

(12-13)…You express a great deal of anxiety over our willingness to break laws. This is certainly a legitimate concern. Since we so diligently urge people to obey the Supreme Court's decision of 1954 outlawing segregation in the public schools, at first glance it may seem rather paradoxical for us consciously to break laws. One may want to ask: "How can you advocate breaking some laws and obeying others?" The answer lies in the fact that there are two types of laws: just and unjust. I would be the first to advocate obeying just laws. One has not only a legal but a moral responsibility to obey just laws. Conversely, one has a moral responsibility to disobey unjust laws. I would agree with St. Augustine that "an unjust law is no law at all."…

— Dr. Martin Luther King Jr.,
"Letter from Birmingham Jail," April 16, 1963

12. Which type of action against unjust laws is Dr. Martin Luther King Jr. supporting in this passage?
    (1) militant resistance
    (2) civil disobedience
    (3) judicial activism
    (4) affirmative action

13. Which statement most accurately summarizes the main idea of the passage?
    (1) People must obey Supreme Court decisions.
    (2) You can never break some laws while obeying others.
    (3) Violence brings faster results than peaceful protest.
    (4) Following moral principles is sometimes more important than following the law.

14. The United States Supreme Court under Chief Justice Earl Warren (1953–1969) made several landmark decisions that
    (1) drew criticism for supporting States rights
    (2) weakened the power of the federal government
    (3) strengthened the authority of the police
    (4) increased the rights of individuals

15. The baby boom after World War II led directly to
    (1) a decrease in spending for public education
    (2) a return to a rural lifestyle
    (3) an increased demand for housing
    (4) a decrease in consumer spending

CHAPTER 22
The Last Forty Years: 1975-2015

158) In the fall of 1969, Richard Nixon, came to power. Riding on a wave of anti-liberal sentiment, Nixon rose to power as young and old conservatives pushed back against the liberalism of the early 60's. Nixon began what has been termed by some as the conservative revolution in American politics.

159) Nixon however looked for a different approach to tackling communism. Nixon pushed for a warming in US-Russian relations which was termed Détente. He was the first sitting President to visit a communist country when he visited China in 1972. However, his presidency was overshadowed (and came to a close) due to his involvement in the Watergate scandal. The scandal began when some thieves broke into a hotel, the Watergate, where democrats were plotting their strategies for the 1972 elections. 5 people were accused of the break in and many had ties to his administration. Accusations surfaced that the President knew about the break in and the subsequent cover up. Despite many battles between the President, Congress and the Supreme Court to stop the secret tapes of his conversations from being released, they were eventually released to the public. Pressure mounted from Congress after official impeachment articles were launched against him, and his ratings fell to 23%. Seeing no way out, Nixon resigned from the presidency. Gerald Ford, the vice president took over after Nixon resigned and pardoned Nixon of any wrongdoing, thus sparing Nixon of any possibility of future prosecution.

160) Ford led the country until he lost in 1976 to President Jimmy Carter. Carter, who came from the South, was a Democrat. Among Carter's lasting achievements was the peace deal he brokered between Israel and Egypt by bringing Prime Minister Menachem Begin (Israel) and President Anwar Sadat (Egypt) to Camp David where the two leaders signed the Camp David accords. He also signed the SALT II Treaty which was designed to lower the number of nuclear weapons that both the US and Russia stockpiled.

161) During his time in office, 444 Americans were taken hostage after the Iranian revolution broke out and the American embassy was taken over. The hostage crisis ended moments after Carter's term was over. It nonetheless weighed heavily on his presidency and was a key reason for his defeat in 1980 against President Reagan. President Carter has been a vocal advocate for human rights since then and an especially vocal critic of Israel.

162) President Reagan, a Republican and staunch conservative, was elected in 1980 to lead the US. He raised the rhetoric against the USSR and built up large stockpiles of weapons resulting in an arms race, a clear reversal of the policies of détente. Reagan mixed heavily into the internal affairs of countries who faced communist insurgencies, launching covert and overt operations against these movements. He advocated the implementation of tax cuts even if that puts us in debt and argued for the supremacy of Supply Side Economics which seeks to lower taxes and decrease government regulation in order to stimulate the economy.

163) During the Reagan administration there were two major scandals: the Iran Contra Affair and the S and L crises. The Iran Contra Affair was a plan by some administration officials to sell weapons to Iran despite the US arms embargo against it. This was done so that they would receive help in releasing 6 American hostages held by Hezbollah. When this was achieved, a high ranking official, Col. Oliver North, diverted some of the money raised by the arms sale to the Contras, an anti-communist force, whose support was banned by Congress. The affair, which was a major headache for the administration, blew over after many crucial documents were destroyed and the administration refused to hand over any other documents in question.

164) The S and L crises was a financial crisis created after many S and L's ("Savings and Loans", a type of fund created by groups of people to help each other get loans for businesses and mortgages) got into other risky investments and lost a lot of their money. Some blamed the President's deregulations as the cause of this crisis.

165) Following Pres. Reagan's two terms in office, his Vice President G.H. Bush became president. Bush senior (or Bush `41 as he is known) played a significant role in the Persian Gulf War in which the US led a coalition to oust Iraqi president Saddam Hussein from Kuwait. It was also during his presidency that the Rodney King race riots broke out in which African American protestors rioted after Rodney King (an African American) was beaten by white Police officers in LA. President Bush also signed into law the Americans With Disabilities Act which provided better public access to handicapped people and made it illegal to discriminate in some cases against people with certain disabilities. It also made it a law that public facilities had to be equipped to handle people with disabilities. Finally, he signed NAFTA (the North American Free Trade Agreement) with Canada, and Mexico which creates a trading bloc between the countries.

166) Following President Bush `41, Democrat Bill Clinton took office. During his two-term presidency, the country's economy roared. Additionally, the internet took off, mobile phone service became commonplace, and the US led a coalition against Slobodan Milosevic in a bid to stop his ethnic cleansing of Bosnia in the 1990's. It also saw the first bombings of the Twin Towers in 1993 by Islamic militants. President Clinton also brought about peace in Northern Ireland and tried mightily to bring peace amongst the Palestinians and Israelis. However, Yasser Arafat, the chief negotiator for the Palestinians walked away from negotiations at the last moment. Clinton also changed the trading relationship with Japan by opening up Japanese markets to American products. Despite his high popularity, Clinton was dogged throughout his long career by allegations of affairs with other women, one which brought impeachment proceedings against him. In the end however, he was cleared by one vote in the senate.

167) Following Clinton's presidency, President George W. Bush (Junior or "W") (2000-2008)

was elected. His election victory over Al Gore was contested and was so close that the Supreme Court needed to rule on who won. Soon after he was elected, 9/11 occurred in which Islamic terrorists brought down the Twin Towers in NYC and hit the Pentagon and a new era the "War on Terror" began. In an attempt to root out regimes which support terror, and to stop Saddam Hussein from proliferating his alleged weapons of mass destruction, the US launched protracted wars against Iraq and Afghanistan which only recently has ended. Also, during his tenure, Hurricane Katrina hit the US which was the costliest natural disaster in the US and killed over 1,000 people. At the end of Mr. Bush's term there was a financial meltdown and recession (called by many the "Great Recession"). This came about after a mortgage crisis in which sub-prime loans were given out to people who couldn't keep up with their mortgage payments caused many banks to lose their money. The government stepped in and supported the banks which helped stabilize the economy and eventually pull back from the brink.

168) Following GW Bush, President Barack Obama, (2008-2016) a democrat, was elected president for two terms. This was a historic election being that Mr. Obama was the first African American President in US History. He was the first President to extensively use social media in getting out the vote and to reach the public in general. He ended the war in Iraq and promised to end the war in Afghanistan. He passed the Affordable Care Act (Obamacare) which granted healthcare to all Americans despite fierce criticism and opposition from the Republican Party. During his first term there was also the BP gulf oil spill- the largest oil spill disaster in the Gulf of Mexico after an oil well under the ocean floor blew up. Under his presidency, massive surveillance by the NSA has been conducted and raised many privacy concerns. Gun control, has also become a national issue after many senseless shootings (called "mass shootings") occurred. Police brutality, especially against African Americans also has arisen and has spawned a new movement called the Black Lives Matter movement.

We leave history at this. Let us see what the future has in store for us.

Fifteen famous Supreme Court decisions

1) Plessey V. Ferguson: (1896) upheld the Jim Crow laws in the south by saying separate but equal is equal.

2) Marbury vs. Madison: (1803) (judicial review, federalism) established Judicial Review after the courts resolved conflicts between branches of government.

3) Dred Scott v. Sanford: (1857) established that slaves were property of their masters and not entitled to civil rights.

4) Brown v. Board of Education of Topeka Kansas: (1954) overturned the Plessey decision and said that separate but equal is unequal

5) Heart of Atlanta Motel v. United States: the US government can use the commerce clause in the constitution to force private businesses to uphold the Civil Rights Act of 1964.

6) Gibbons v. Ogden: (1824) determined that the commerce clause in the constitution grants the federal government the right in deciding how interstate commerce should run.

7) Tinker v. Des Moines: (1969) schools cannot restrict free speech without good reasons.

8) McCulloch v. Maryland: (1819) established the right of the federal government to tax and override states objections to national projects (such as the national bank in that case)

9) Korematsu v. United States: (1944) ruled that state security overrides any particular American citizen's rights.

10) Mapp v. Ohio: (1961) a search that comes up with materials to convict, that was done without a search warrant, is inadmissible in court

11) Gideon v. Wainwright: (1963) A state court must provide a person with a lawyer if they cannot afford one.

12) Miranda v. Arizona: (1966) a person must be read their "right to remain silent" when facing conviction.

13) Roe v. Wade: (1973) grants people the right to an abortion

14) United States V. Nixon: (1974) executive privilege is not limitless

15) Regents of the University of California V. Bakke: (1978) (Affirmative action) excluded race based admissions exclusively but allowed race to play a role in admissions

REGENTS REVIEW

>...Just over a month ago, General Secretary Gorbachev [of the Soviet Union and I met for the first time in Geneva. Our purpose was to begin a fresh chapter in the relations between our two countries and to try to reduce the suspicions and mistrust between us. I think we made a good beginning. Mr. Gorbachev and I spent many hours together, speaking frankly and seriously about the most important issues of our time: reducing the massive nuclear arsenals on both sides, resolving regional conflicts, ensuring respect for human rights as guaranteed under international agreements, and other questions of mutual interest. As the elected representative of the American people, I told Mr. Gorbachev of our deep desire for peace and that the American people do not wish the Soviet people any harm....
> — President Ronald Reagan, January 1, 1986

1. One major issue that dominated United States–Soviet relations at this time was the
    (1) war in Southeast Asia
    (2) use of apartheid in South Africa
    (3) danger of nuclear destruction
    (4) threat from al Qaeda in the Middle East (Aug. '12, 41, 42, 43, 49)

2. Passage of the Americans with Disabilities Act (1990) improved conditions for the disabled by
    (1) making it illegal to criticize or fire handicapped persons
    (2) mandating easier access to employment and public facilities
    (3) sponsoring Olympic games for the handicapped
    (4) requiring separate classrooms for disabled students

>...After 20 months of negotiations, I ordered my Trade Representative, Ambassador Kantor, to impose sanctions on Japan unless they agreed to open these markets. Today Japan has agreed that it will begin to truly open its auto and auto parts markets to American companies....
> — President Bill Clinton, Remarks on the Japan–United States Trade Agreement, June 28, 1995

3. President Clinton's actions were a reaction to
    (1) an ongoing trade deficit with Japan
    (2) a threat of war with Japan
    (3) the refusal of Japan to import Alaskan oil
    (4) tension over having to protect Japan from Chinese aggression

4. **Which development led to the other three?**
   - (1) United States invasion of Afghanistan
   - (2) increased security at airports
   - (3) creation of the Department of Homeland Security
   - (4) September 11, 2001 attacks on the United States

5. **A valid generalization about Presidential elections since 1960 is that**
   - (1) campaign finance laws have reduced spending by candidates
   - (2) most of the winning candidates have come from New England
   - (3) more than 90 percent of eligible voters have participated in each election
   - (4) candidates have used new forms of mass media to reach voters

6. **The Strategic Arms Limitation Treaty (SALT), signed by President Richard Nixon with the Soviet Union, was an effort to advance the foreign policy of**
   - (1) détente
   - (2) imperialism
   - (3) brinkmanship
   - (4) globalization (June `12, 39, 41, 47, 48)

7. **One unique feature of the Presidential election of 2000 between George W. Bush and Al Gore is that**
   - (1) the Supreme Court played an important role in the final outcome
   - (2) no third-party candidate was on the ballot
   - (3) both candidates had previously served as vice President
   - (4) the electoral votes in Florida were divided between the candidates

8. **The terms Teapot Dome, Watergate, and Iran-Contra are most closely associated with**
   - (1) domestic policies
   - (2) Presidential scandals
   - (3) federal court decisions
   - (4) failed reform movements

9. **One way in which the New Deal and the Great Society are similar is that both programs were based on the belief that**
   - (1) volunteer organizations should take over federal relief efforts
   - (2) government should impose fewer regulations on business
   - (3) states should pay a larger share of the cost of federal programs
   - (4) the federal government should do more to help citizens in need

10. A main goal of President Richard Nixon's policy of détente was to
    (1) sponsor free elections in North and South Korea
    (2) reduce tensions between the United States and the Soviet Union
    (3) negotiate an end to the Arab-Israeli conflict
    (4) build support for recognition of the Nationalist government of Taiwan

11. President Ronald Reagan asked Congress to lower tax rates on businesses and wealthy individuals in order to
    (1) encourage new economic investment
    (2) increase exports to Asia
    (3) impose limits on the money supply
    (4) preserve funds for social welfare programs

(12-13)…Keeping America competitive requires affordable energy. And here we have a serious problem: America is addicted to oil, which is often imported from unstable parts of the world. The best way to break this addiction is through technology. Since 2001, we have spent nearly $10 billion to develop cleaner, cheaper, and more reliable alternative energy sources. And we are on the threshold of incredible advances.…
— President George W. Bush,
State of the Union Address, January 31, 2006

12. In this passage, President George W. Bush suggests Americans can overcome oil "addiction" by focusing on
    (1) conservation
    (2) education
    (3) scientific research
    (4) discovery of new oil fields

13. Which goal related to United States energy needs is addressed in this speech?
    (1) reduce dependence on the Middle East
    (2) supply all energy needs from domestic sources
    (3) decrease offshore drilling
    (4) eliminate the use of all petroleum

14. Leaders of the Progressive movement, the New Deal, and the Great Society shared the common belief that the United States government should
    (1) increase its involvement in the economy to improve people's lives
    (2) strengthen the reserved powers of the states
    (3) provide for racial equality for all people
    (4) support laissez-faire business practices

"President Lincoln Declares Martial Law"
"President Roosevelt Issues Executive Order to Detain Japanese Americans"
"President Bush Orders Terrorist Suspects Held at Guantanamo"

15. These headlines best demonstrate that
    (1) the system of checks and balances equalizes the powers of governmental branches
    (2) Presidential power often increases during times of crisis
    (3) Presidents act forcefully during periods of economic depression
    (4) Presidential decisions made to resolve national crises are rarely controversial

16. Which action was a major foreign policy achievement of President Jimmy Carter?
    (1) settling the Suez crisis
    (2) withdrawing the United States from the Vietnam War
    (3) establishing improved relations with Iran
    (4) mediating the Camp David Accords between Egypt and Israel

17. President Ronald Reagan used the concept of supply-side economics when he proposed
    (1) reducing income taxes to stimulate growth
    (2) providing direct payments to people living in poverty
    (3) creating government jobs to keep people working
    (4) increasing regulations on business to promote Competition

18. How is the Presidential election of 2000 similar to the Presidential elections of 1824 and 1876?
    (1) The electoral vote count ended in a tie.
    (2) The third-party candidate won several electoral votes.
    (3) The winner of the popular vote did not become President.
    (4) The United States Senate selected the winner.

19. A major way in which the Civil Rights Act (1964) and the Americans with Disabilities Act (1990) are similar is that both laws
    (1) were intended to lift Americans out of poverty
    (2) failed to pass Constitutional review by the Supreme Court
    (3) gave a minority group the right to vote after years of protest
    (4) provided equal protection to groups that had experienced discrimination

20. What was one result of the Supreme Court's decision in Gibbons v. Ogden (1824)?
    (1) The power of the federal government over interstate commerce was strengthened.
    (2) The rights of accused individuals were expanded.
    (3) The power of the judicial branch was limited.
    (4) The Court declined to hear cases involving disputes between states

Answer Key

1) 1 see entry # 2
2) 4 see entry # 2
3) 1 being that canals nor railroads nor turnpikes existed before the 1800's and so the only answer left is rivers.

Answer Key: Slave issues
1) 4 see entry # 6 for triangular trade

Answer key: Democratic Foundations
1) 4 see entry # 9a-b for the Virginia house of burgesses
2) 2 see entry # 8a for declaration of independence
3) 4 see entry # 8a-c for these thinkers and their influence
4) 4 see entry # 7 last bullet for habeas corpus
5) 2 see entry # 9a-b for Virginia house of burgesses

Answer key: Revolutionary Rumblings
1) 1 see entry # 10 on Mercantilism
2) 2 see entry # 12-17 on laws and responses
3) 4 see entry # 15 on Thomas Paine and common sense
4) 2 see entry # 12 on boycotts

Answer key: revolution
1) 1 this is the only economic (having to do with money) weakness listed also see entry # 23b for weakness in A of C
2) 2 the other choices were never found in the A of C but rather in the Constitution
3) 4 see entry # 22b for Northwest Ordinance
4) 1 see entry # 21 for purpose of A of C

Answer Key: From Revolution to Statehood
1) 3 see entry # 28 and 29 for entries on both compromises on slavery and representation
2) 2 see entry #24 and 25-since the rebellion needed a federal response which the government was unprepared the government responded by scrapping the A of C due to its weaknesses.
3) 4 see entry # 29 on 3/5ths compromise- being that the southern states relied so heavily on slavery they opposed any efforts by the North to rid the US of slavery and even wanted them placed legally in the Constitution.

Answer key: the Legislative Branch
1) 4 see entry # 31 on the concept of separation of powers and the resulting Balance of Power
2) 2 see entry # 31 on the Preamble
3) 2 see entry # 31 on the concept of separation of powers and the resulting Balance of Power

Answer Key: the Executive branch
1) 1 see entry # 46 (redo) on unwritten Constitution
2) 1 see entry # 46
3) 3 see entry # 46

Answer Key: The Judicial Branch
1) 4 see entry "the republican form of government to see this point being made

which is seen as unfair since it means that one may lose the popular vote while winning the election
2) 1 see entry # 51 on Judicial review
3) 4 see entry # 52 on the Bill of Rights
4) 3 only B and D are confident that the Constitution as it is will be an Ok system of governance. Speaker b because he says that the separation of powers will provide check and balance while speaker D says that we can always change the Constitution as the needs arise.
5) 4 see entry # 51 on Judicial review
6) 3 see entry # 51 on Federalism
7) 2 see entry # 51 on Judicial review
8) 3 see entry # 52 and 26 where it discusses the federalist papers
9) 1 as seen from the affects of Judicial review

Answer Key: Post Constitutional America 1791-1820
1) 3 see entry # 56 on Washington's farewell address
2) 1 see entry # 53b and 54 on elastic clause
3) 1 see entry # 53-54 on elastic clause
4) 1 see entry # 53c on whiskey rebellion
5) 3 see entry # 55, 57 on war of 1812
6) 4 see entry # 53b and 54 for loose interpretation
7) 2 see entry # 59 on Monroe Doctrine
8) 4 see entry # 53b-54 for debate of loose constructionist
9) 2 see entry # 53b-54 on debate which led to political parties

Answer Key: America 1810-1830
1) 3 see entry # 67 for more on the Louisiana Purchase
2) 2 see entry # 64 for more on the spoils system
3) 3 see entry # 62 for more on immigration
4) 2 see entry # 60 for more on the impact of the Erie canal
5) 3 see entry # 66 for more on the trail of tears and Worcester Vs. Georgia
6) 3 see entry # 67 for more on the Louisiana purchase
7) 3 see entry # 60 for more info on the Erie Canal

Answer key: Reform and Growth: America 1830's-1860's
1) 1 see entry # 69 for more on manifest Destiny
2) 2 see entry # 72 on the Kansas-Nebraska act and see entry # for more info on Popular sovereignty
3) 4 see entry # 73 for more info on the 14th amendment
4) 1 see entry # 68 for more info on Prohibition
5) 1 see entry # 72 see more info on causes of civil war
6) 4 see entry #74-75 for more info on reconstruction debates
7) 1 see entry # 68 for more on Prohibition
8) 4 all the above occurred during the civil war including his reelection in 1864 see entry # 73
9) 1 see entry # 72 for more on the various attempts at peace making over slavery
10) 3 after the civil war the attempted assertion by the states of state's rights (at least to secede from the Union) was doomed and the power of the federal government increased
11) 4 see entry # 68 on prohibition

Answer key: Reconstruction-1865-1877
1) 3 see entry # 75 on sharecropping-this was a relatively cheap way of keeping down labor costs
2) 3 see entry # 83 on Plessey Vs. Ferguson
3) 2 see entry # 75 on sharecropping
4) 3 see entry # 82 on Jim crow laws
5) 2 see entry # 82 on Jim crow Laws

6) 1 see entry # 81 on end of reconstruction
7) 3 see entry # 83 on Plessey Vs. Ferguson
8) 4 see entry # 74 on Lincolns approach to reconstruction
9) 1 see entry # 81 on end of reconstruction
10) 2 see entry # 82 on Literacy tests and grandfather clause

Answer key: The Growth of American business: 1880-1920
1) 2 see entry # 88 for robber baron
2) 4 see entry # 85-86 on business growth
3) 3 see entry # 91 on AFL
4) 4 see entry # 89 on social Darwinism
5) 1 see entry # 91 on AFL
6) 3 see entry # 91 on formation of Labor Unions

Urbanization and immigration:1880's-1920's
1) 4 since these two are both opinions while other two are facts about the times
2) 2 see entry # 97 on new immigration
3) 2 see entry # 100 on the Grange movement
4) 3 the clue is in the words abundant crop raised everywhere..
5) 1 see entry # 100 on the populist party
6) 1 see entry # 97 on Nativism and the gentleman's agreement and the Chinese exclusion act
7) 4 see entry # 97 on Nativism
8) 3 see entry # 93 on urbanization
9) 1 see entry # 97 on nativism

Answer Key: The progressive movement: 1880's-1920's
1) 1 see entry # 109 on conservation
2) 2 see entry # 102 on Muckrakers and their impact
3) 4 see entry # 102 on Muckraking
4) 1 see entry # 102on the meat inspection act
5) 1 see entry # 108 on direct elections of Senators which reduced the influence of wealthy patrons who friends with state legislators who put the senators in office
6) 2 see entry # 102on Sinclair Lewis
7) 3 see entry # 109on square deal
8) 3 see entry # 102 on Muckraking
9) 1 see entry # 111on Federal reserve
10) 3 see entry # 111on graduated income tax
11) 1 see entry # 107on ADL and NAACP
12) 1 see entry # 109-110on trust busting
13) 4 see entry # 102 on famous Muckrakers
14) 3 see entry # 105 on the temperance movement

Answer key: The Imperialistic age: 1880's-1920's
1) 1 see entry # 116 on yellow journalism
2) 4 see entry # 118 on the Roosevelt corollary to the Monroe Doctrine
3) 4 see entry # 116 on yellow journalism
4) 2 see entry # 113 for reasons for imperialism
5) 3 see entry # 116 on yellow journalism

Answer Key: WWI and the interwar years: 1917-1941
1) 4 see entry # 123 for the defeat of the treaty of Versailles in the senate
2) 2 see entry # 125 for entry on causes of the great depression
3) 3 see entry # 124 for the Harlem Renaissance
4) 3 see entry # 124 for the red scare and the trial of Vanzetti and Sacco
5) 3 see entry # 125 for the causes of the great depression
6) 3 see entry # 121 for the case of Schenk V. United states
7) 4 see entry # 121 for Wilson and his role in the economy
8) 3 see entry # 123 for reasons the Versailles treaty was rejected in the US Senate
9) 2 see entry # 124 for the scopes trial and the end of prohibition in # 68

American History Regents Review | 97

10) 4 see entry # 125 for the dust bowl
11) 4 see entry # 120 for the Zimmerman note
12) 2 see entry # 120 for reasons the US got into the first world war
13) 3 see entry # 123 for reasons the US senate rejected the Versailles treaty
14) 1 see entry # 124 for the great migration
15) 3 see entry # 124 for the Harlem renaissance
16) 2 see entry # 120 for the US involvement in WWI
17) 1 see entry # 123 for the US rejection of the Versailles treaty

Answer Key: The new Deal and WWII: 1930-1945

1) 4 see entry # 123, and 130 on US isolationist attitudes between the two wars
2) 1 see entry # 130 on the bombing of Japan
3) 2 see entry # 132 on the Nuremberg trials
4) 1 see entry # 128 on the role of the government during the depression
5) 2 see entry # 130 on US involvement in WWII before Pearl Harbor
6) 3 see entry # 132 on Nuremberg trials
7) 2 see entry # 129 on court packing
8) 3 see entry # 135 on rationing and price controls
9) 4 see entry # 134 on Japanese internment caps
10) 4 see entry # 135 on rationing
11) 3 see entry # 130 the atomic bomb
12) 4 see entry # 133 on women involvement in WWII
13) 1 see entry # 134 on Japanese internment camps

Answer Key: The Cold War: 1945-1990

1) 2 see entry # 144 on the launch of Sputnik
2) 3 see entry # 137 on Berlin airlift
3) 1 see entry # 141 on Senator McCarthy
4) 3 see entry # 136 on the purpose of the UN
5) 4 see entry # 144 on the launch of Sputnik
6) 3 see entry # 139 on the Marshall Plan
7) 2 see entry # on the U2 incident # 143 and the Cuban missile crisis # 143
8) 4 see entry # 141 on the Rosenberg's and the Palmer raids # 125

Answer Key: 1945-1975: economic, social and cultural change

1) 3 see entry # 147 on the growth of the suburbs
2) 4 see entry # 149 on the decision by Governor Faubus not to allow de-segregation
3) 2 see entry # 149 on the Little Rock incident
4) 3 see entry # 157 on the Great war on poverty
5) 2 see entry # 146 on the GI bill
6) 2 see entry # 149 on the Brown V. the Board of education of Topeka Kansas
7) 2 see entry # 149 the little rock nine
8) 4 see entry # 151 on civil disobedience
9) 4 see entry # 156 on the generation gap
10) 4 see entry # 147 on the growth of the suburbs
11) 1 see entry # 156 on the peace corps
12) 2 see entry # 151 on civil disobedience
13) 4 obvious from the response of Dr. King that if a law is moral one needs to keep it while if it is not one should not keep it
14) 4 see entry # 153 on Roe V Wade
15) 3 see entry #146 on baby boom. Naturally more people means an increase in the need for more housing

Answer Key: The last 40 years: 1975-2005

1) 3 see entry #160 on nuclear Proliferation and SALT II treaty

2) 2 see entry #165 on the disabilities act
3) 1 see entry # 166 on trade deficits with Japan
4) 4 see entry # 167 on 9/11 attacks
5) 4 with the new media new ways of reaching voters has come about
6) 1 see entry # 159 on detente
7) 1 see entry # 167 on the 2000 Presidential election
8) 2 see entry # 159 on Watergate
9) 4 see entry # 157 on the Great Society
10) 2 see entry # on détente
11) 1 see entry # on Reagans supply side economics
12) 3 as he states-through scientific invention we will overcome our oil addiction
13) 1 obvious from the paragraph
14) 1 see entry # 157 on the great society
15) 2 as seen from all the above-the power of the President increases as by withholding free speech etc.
16) 4 see entry # 160 on the Camp David accords
17) 1 see entry # 162 on supply side economics
18) 3 see entry # 167 on Presidential elections of 2000
19) 4 see entry # 165 on the disabilities act

www.ingramcontent.com/pod-product-compliance
Lightning Source LLC
Chambersburg PA
CBHW081353080526
44588CB00016B/2487